Assessment of Health and Physical Education

Assessment of Health and Physical Education

George K. Mathews

CRESCENT
PUBLISHING CORPORATION

[*The responsibility for the facts stated, conclusions reached and plagiarism, if any, in this book is entirely that of the Author. And the Publisher bears no responsibility for them, whatsoever.*]

Assessment of Health and Physical Education

First Published : 2009

ISBN 978-81-8342-125-6

Published by :

CRESCENT PUBLISHING CORPORATION
4831/24, Prahlad Street,
Ansari Road, Darya Ganj,
New Delhi - 110002
Ph. : 23272541, 23257835
Fax : 91- 011- 23257835
e-mail : campusbooks@hotmail.com

Printed at :
Roshan Offset Printers
Delhi

Preface

Physical education is the process that uses physical activity as a means to help people acquire skills, health, fitness, knowledge and attitudes that contribute to their optimal development and wellbeing. It plays an important role in the development of an individual just as a school room education does. Hence, it is important that physical education be incorporated along with a student's curriculum.

Physical education is considered a supplement to the learner's growing value system. One of its aims is to expand options for wise use of leisure time. Taking up a regular physical activity is a health-enhancing move. The physical education schedule must be developed in accordance with a variety of factors. The age of the individual is a very crucial consideration when chalking out such a schedule. The physical educator must be responsible enough to help the learner develop the ability to choose wisely when it comes to making decisions about physical activity be it in the present or in the future. The objectives of physical education include getting the individual to achieve his or her highest competency in movement skills.

Individual and team sports, dance, aquatics, gymnastics, and fitness activities designed to develop beginning and intermediate skills are all part of physical education curriculum. Most schools have comprehensive physical education programs. One advantage of such programs is that it instills at a very young age the need for exercise and fitness in life. Young children such as pre-schoolers and first graders can be made to participate in healthy outdoor activities with an element of fun added to the schedule. This makes the experience interesting for both the students and the teacher.

The teachers should qualified and trained in this field. A physical education teacher is also required to have basic knowledge of diet and nutrition so he or she can help students structure a nutritious food chart to supplement their physical training. A good training program and substantial diet can go a long way in ensuring fitness and health for many years to come.

This book assess the new trends and issues the field of physical education. The contents of the book will help physical education teachers and coaches to tackle specific problems of the sportspersons. The language used is simple and is within the comprehension level of teachers and students pursuing career in physical and sports.

George K. Mathews

Contents

1

Standards for Health and Physical Education

The most major health problems in the world today are caused by six categories of behavior: behaviors that lead to intentional and unintentional injuries; smoking; alcohol and other drug use; sexual behaviors leading to sexually transmitted diseases, HIV infection, and unintended pregnancy; poor nutrition; and lack of physical activity. Behaviors and attitudes about health that are initiated during childhood are responsible for most of the leading causes of death, illness, and disability in the Uunited States today. Comprehensive school health education programs represent one effective way of providing students with the knowledge and skills to prevent health-impairing behaviors.

Hundreds of studies have evaluated health education and concluded that it is effective in reducing the number of teenage pregnancies, decreasing smoking rates among young people, and preventing the adoption of many high-risk behaviors. But its effectiveness depends upon factors such as teacher training, comprehensiveness of the health program, time available for instruction, family involvement, and community support. And, sequential school health education programs for students have been found to be more effective in changing health behaviors than occasional programs on single health topics.

The Louis Harris survey of over 4,700 students in grades 3 through 12 who were attending 199 public schools found that health knowledge, attitudes, and behaviors improved with increasing years of health instruction. The School Health Education Evaluation, which looked at four different health curricula for 30,000 4th through 7th graders in 20 states, found:

— Students receiving health instruction had higher knowledge scores than students with no health instruction, with the greatest differences seen in knowledge of substance use and abuse;

— Knowledge, attitudes, and skills improved even with minimal instruction, but gains were most apparent when students received at least 50 hours of health instruction per school year; and

— More hours were needed to improve attitudes than to enhance health knowledge and practices.

In USA, to assist schools in developing and evaluating comprehensive health education programs, the Joint Committee for National School Health Education Standards has developed guidelines for school health standards. The committee was made up of representatives from the Association for the Advancement of Health Education, the American Public Health Association, the American School Health Association, and the Society of State Directors of Health, Physical Education and Recreation and was sponsored by the American Cancer Society.

The committee's goal was to emphasize the need for school health education and create a framework for local school boards to use in determining content of the health curriculum in their communities. There are seven broad standards that promote health literacy, which is the capacity of individuals to obtain, interpret, and understand basic health information and services and the competence to use such information and services in ways which enhance health. For each standard there are performance indicators to help educators determine the knowledge and skills that students should possess by the end of grades 4, 8, and 11.

— *Standard 1*: Students will comprehend concepts related to health promotion and disease prevention. Performance indicators for this standard center around identifying what good health is, recognizing health problems, and ways in which lifestyle, the environment, and public policies can promote health.

— *Standard 2*: Students will demonstrate the ability to access valid health information and health-promoting products and services. Performance indicators focus on identification of valid health information, products, and services including advertisements, health insurance and treatment options, and food labels.

— *Standard 3*: Students will demonstrate the ability to practice health-enhancing behaviors and reduce health risks. Performance indicators include identifying responsible and harmful behaviors, developing health-enhancing strategies, and managing stress.

— *Standard 4*: Students will analyze the influence of culture, media, technology, and other factors on health. Performance indicators are related to describing and analyzing how one's cultural background, messages from the media, technology, and one's friends influence health.

— *Standard 5*: Students will demonstrate the ability to use interpersonal communication skills to enhance health. Performance indicators relate to interpersonal communication, refusal and negotiation skills, and conflict resolution.

— *Standard 6*: Students will demonstrate the ability to use goal-setting and decision-making skills to enhance health. Performance indicators focus on setting reasonable and attainable goals and developing positive decision-making skills.

— *Standard 7*: Students will demonstrate the ability to advocate for personal, family, and community health. Performance indicators relate to identifying community resources, accurately communicating health information and ideas, and working cooperatively to promote health.

Curriculum Content

The school health education program should be based upon local needs—the health behaviors and problems within the school population—and national data suggesting the health status of children and youth. Experts have identified 10 content areas as necessary for a comprehensive school health education program:

— community health

— consumer health

— environmental health

— personal health and fitness

— family life education

— nutrition and healthy eating

— disease prevention and control

— safety and injury prevention

— prevention of substance use and abuse (alcohol, tobacco, drugs)

— growth and development

The objective is to offer an ongoing, sequenced, and developmentally appropriate program that is consistent with community needs and providing at least 50 hours per year of health instruction. Some references for identifying curricula are listed at the end of this Digest.

Teaching Practices

At the elementary and middle school level, the classroom teacher is expected to teach health as a curricular area like math, reading, and social studies. At the high school level, 39 states require that health be taught by a teacher who is certified in health education. Many teachers avoid health subjects because of inadequate undergraduate training.

The most effective methods of instruction in health are student-centered approaches: hands-on activities, cooperative learning techniques, and activities that include problem-solving and peer instruction to help students develop skills in decision-making, communication, setting goals, resistance to peer pressure, and stress management. As with other instructional areas, the teacher should promote parental involvement by sending materials home, involving parents in classroom activities, and creating assignments that involve parents.

Because of time limitations in the school day, some teachers find it helpful to infuse health topics into other subject areas. For example, a unit on smoking might include:

— investigating the effects of smoking on body systems (science);

— developing, administering, and analyzing a survey on student attitudes about smoking (math);

— writing an antismoking advertisement (language arts);

— examining the economics of smoking in states where tobacco is a significant crop (social studies).

Teacher Preparation

Teacher preparation is critical to successful school health education programs. If children and youth are to achieve health literacy, teacher preparation programs will need to support preservice health education that addresses:

— health content

— teaching methods for teacher education

— including health content across the curriculum

— cultural diversity of teachers and students

— assessment of student achievement

Standards for Physical Education

Physical education is an integral part of the total education of the child and virtually every state, district, and school requires physical education for its students. Quality physical education programs are needed to increase the physical competence, health-related fitness, self-esteem, and enjoyment of physical activity for all students so that they can be physically active for a lifetime. Knowing that physical activity promotes health is not enough: students must be given opportunities to gain the knowledge and skills needed to adopt active lifestyles.

Physical activity improves muscular strength and endurance, flexibility, and cardiovascular endurance, as well as serves as a vehicle that helps children establish self-esteem and strive for achievable, personal goals. The Surgeon General's report, Physical Activity and Health concludes that regular moderate physical activity can substantially reduce the risk of developing or dying from heart disease, diabetes, colon cancer, and high blood pressure. The American Heart Association ecommends that all children aged 5 years or older should engage in at least 30 minutes of daily physical activity at a moderate intensity and vigorous physical activity for 30 minutes at least 3 days per week.

Acknowledgment of the contributions of school physical education to health led to the inclusion of two national objectives that are related to school physical education in Healthy People 2000, the U.S. Department of Health and Human Services national health objectives:

— Increase to at least 50% the proportion of children and adolescents in grades 1-12 who participate in daily school physical education.

— Increase to at least 50% the proportion of school physical education class time that students spend being physically active, preferably engaged in lifetime physical activities.

The Surgeon General's report calls school-based physical education "the most widely available resource for promoting physical activity among young people in the United States," and recommends that "every effort should be made to encourage schools to require daily physical education in each grade and to promote physical activities that can be enjoyed throughout life."

In US, the National Association for Sport and Physical Education (NASPE) appointed its Outcomes Committee in 1986 to answer the question, "What should physically educated students know and be able to do?" The result of the Outcomes Project was a definition that includes five major focus areas, specifying that a physically educated person:

— has learned skills necessary to perform a variety of physical activities,

— is physically fit,

— participates regularly in physical activity,

— knows the implications of and the benefits from involvement in physical activities,

— values physical activity and its contribution to a healthful lifestyle.

Following the work of the Outcomes Committee, a Standards and Assessment Task Force was appointed to develop content standards and assessment material based on the previous work. The standards document developed by this group had the following purposes:

— to establish content standards for the physical education school program that clearly identify consensus statements related to what a student should know and be able to do as a result of a quality physical education program; and

— to establish teacher-friendly guidelines for assessment of the content standards that are consistent with instructionally integrated orientations toward the role of assessment in teaching and learning.

In "Moving into the Future: National Standards for Physical Education, A Guide to Content and Assessment," a general description of each content standard is first presented, followed by presentation of the standards according to grade level: K, 2, 4, 6, 8, 10, and 12. Within each grade level, the standard is further defined, followed by a listing of the key points of emphasis for that grade level. Sample performance benchmarks, which describe developmentally appropriate behaviors representative of progress toward achieving the standard, are also presented. Lastly, a variety of assessment techniques appropriate for assessing student achievement of the specified content standard is described.

The US National Standards for Physical Education indicate that a physically educated student:

1. Demonstrates competency in many movement forms and proficiency in a few movement forms.
2. Applies involvement concepts and principles to the learning and development of motor skills.
3. Exhibits a physically active lifestyle.
4. Achieves and maintains a health-enhancing level of physical fitness.
5. Demonstrates responsible personal and social behavior in physical activity settings.
6. Demonstrates understanding and respect for differences among people in physical activity settings.
7. Understands that physical activity provides opportunities for enjoyment, challenge, self-expression, and social interaction.

Since 1850, when the first physical training of students in schools began, the emphasis of school physical education has expanded from physical training and calisthenics to performance-related fitness and the development of competitive sports skills. Today the focus of contemporary physical education is on health-related fitness and the behavioral competencies and motor skills needed for lifelong engagement in healthy and satisfying physical activity.

A quality physical education curriculum includes:

— mastery of basic skills and understanding of motor skills related to a variety of physical activities so that each individual can make positive decisions about physical activity choices;

— experiences that encourage children to question, integrate, analyze, communicate, and apply cognitive concepts about motor skill and physical activity;

— opportunities to improve social and cooperative skills, and gain a respect and appreciation for diversity; and

— use of fitness education and assessment to help children understand, enjoy, improve, and/or maintain their physical health and well-being.

To maximize the opportunities to learn in physical education, a range of factors must be available. These include time in the schedule, reasonable class size, adequate facilities and equipment, a well-planned curriculum, appropriate assessment procedures, qualified teachers, and positive administrative support.

In the continuing quest to make physical education experiences more personally relevant to children and youth, new developments in learning theories, structuring of subject matter, and new perceptions concerning growth and development must be continuously considered, evaluated, and implemented. The teacher plays the central role in the success of a physical education program and priority must be given to employing qualified elementary, middle, and secondary school physical education teachers to maximize student learning and achievement.

Quality physical education is both developmentally and instructionally appropriate for the specific children being served. Instructionally appropriate physical education incorporates the best known practices, derived from research and experiences in teaching children, into a program that maximizes opportunities for learning and success for all. Students should also use technology in today s physical education classes to explore fitness and motor skill concepts in ways that personalize the curriculum more than ever before. Heart rate monitors, video and digital photography, computer software, and equipment to measure body composition are a few of the tools made possible by technology. Teacher preparation is critical to successful school physical education programs.

NASPE standards for beginning physical education teachers outline standards in nine areas: content knowledge, growth and development, diverse learners, management and motivation, communication, planning and instruction, learner assessment, reflection, and collaboration. These standards provide the basis for guidelines for professional preparation of physical education teachers who have sound knowledge and understanding of kinesiology (the content of physical education) and are also knowledgeable and skillful in the pedagogy that is needed to transmit this knowledge to students.

Quality physical education programs taught by well-trained physical education specialists play a significant role in promoting the health of children and, ultimately, adults. The National Physical Education Standards provide a framework for structuring programs that will develop physically educated children to help the nation to reach its health goals for children and adults.

2

Benefits of Physical Activity

Regular physical activity has a number of proven, positive health effects, especially on heart health. Vigorous exercise strengthens the heart as a pump, making it a larger, more efficient muscle. Even moderate activity can boost cholesterol, aid the circulatory system, and lower blood pressure and blood fats. All these effects translate into reduced risk for heart disease, heart attack, and stroke. Exercise can also offer other benefits, including strengthened muscles, increased flexibility, and stronger bones, which can help ward off the bone-thinning condition called osteoporosis. Regular activity also promises mental-health benefits, like relieving stress and anxiety. It can help you sleep better and renew your energy. If exercise could be bottled, it would be a best-selling potion at the local pharmacy.

Virtually everyone can get health benefits from activity. But every few years, surveys confirm the well-known fact that most people aren't active enough. Unfortunately, we pay for it. The reasons for inactivity aren't hard to figure out. Most of us have jobs where we sit most of the time, so chances are limited to be physically active at work. We also rely heavily on modern, labor-saving devices - cars, appliances, and power tools - to spare us manual effort.

But there's another reason why many people, especially the overweight, avoid activity. Check out the firm, supple bodies shown exercising on television or on magazine covers. They give the impression that exercise is sweaty, strenuous work best reserved for the young, super-fit, and athletic. But the latest research is proving that picture false: Benefits can be gained even from low-intensity activity, like gardening.

If you burn more calories than you consume, then you'll shed pounds. For every extra 3,500 calories you spend, you'll drop one pound. Do strenuous exercise, and you'll burn calories in a hurry. And you can burn the same number of calories with gentler activity: You just have to do it longer and/or more often. If you're not familiar with the number of calories burned during exercise, you may be discouraged when you first learn about it. For instance, if you weigh 150 pounds and go on a brisk, 1-mile walk for 20 minutes, you'll expend about 100 calories, considerably short of the 3,500 calories needed to drop a pound. But such efforts add up. If you expend an extra 300 calories a day through activity and reduce your dietary intake another 200 calories, then by the end of a week, you'll have a calorie deficit of 3,500, comparable to a one-pound weight loss. This is precisely the kind of gradual success that experts recommend for long-term weight management.

Exercise also has other body-slimming effects. It builds muscle and displaces fat. A given volume of muscle weighs more than the same bulk of fat. So your bathroom scale may not record dramatic changes, but your clothes will be looser, and you'll have a trimmer body shape. Because exercise builds muscle, it may also help counter a problem caused by dieting. When you reduce calories, your body metabolism may slack off and burn calories more slowly. This makes further weight loss more difficult. But some research suggests regular activity helps correct this slowdown and makes it easier to keep shedding pounds.

The more active you are, the more calories you'll burn, which can help with weight loss. And exercise also promotes fat loss and builds muscle. This, in turn, increases your body's metabolic rate, the rate at which you burn calories, even after you've finished exercising.

Weight loss by reducing your calorie intake without activity can have just the opposite effect: It can cause your body to break down muscle, which ultimately lowers your metabolic rate and makes losing weight even harder.

The problem of reducing your calorie intake without exercise is compounded when people go off their diets. Because they've lost muscle, they tend to regain their weight quickly and then some.

A better approach is to increase activity, which builds muscle, at the same time that you're cutting back on excess calories from food. Physical activity can also reduce stress and regulate your appetite, making it easier to curb the urge to overeat.

The amount of energy needed for any activity, whether it's raking leaves or playing a computer game, depends on three factors: your muscle mass, your body weight, and the activity itself. The larger the muscle mass and heavier the body part being moved, the more calories you use. The duration, frequency, and intensity of exercise also count.

Trends in Physical Training

Playing is the fundamental right of a child, either in school or outside. The children, after school, make their own teams with the locally available friends, choose a game of their liking, devise rules and play the game to their heart's content. They tactfully deal with the idea of referee and penalty for infringement of rules. The main idea behind such games is that the children enjoy playing, they make friends, they play as teams and, such play is to provide them with lot of challenging opportunities to provide their talents and fun. The most important factor here is that we could not overlook an outsider, even as the teacher or a coach or a leader does not control the children. When this is possible without a leader, a teacher or a coach outside the school, why is it that such things are not happening in the school where physical education is compulsory for all and a physical education teacher is available?

In most of the schools in India, the physical education teachers are manning the classes from six and above. Such a teacher is to manage a minimum of 100 children at a time within a limited space of the playground surrounded by houses, bushes and filthy waste dumps. What happens to the children of classes three, four and five? They are given to class teachers with the timetable marked by physical training. What do they do? They simply use such periods for correction work and keep the children idle under trees. Some teachers choose class leaders and ask them to give some exercise regimen under a tree outside a classroom while the teacher minds his/her business of correction.

Beyond the sixth standard, the physical education teacher is unable to man the whole lot of 100 and more children. The teacher decides what the children should play and gives them some instructions to play. Many children slowly get dejected without getting even a single chance to play and walk out of the field to the shady place to spend their time idly. This is a common sight in almost all the schools. Why? No one is accountable in the side of physical education. No testing, no evaluation and no follow-up. Many physical education teachers are unsuccessful in their attempts to do some thing novel. No one is interested in this field.

The people who talk a lot on education, fail to understand the delicate line of difference between academics and physical education. They turn down the fact that children could learn whatever they learn in academics through physical education, rejecting the idea that the children would derive the basic values through physical education. The interest of the children is neglected. The teachers dominate the classes and the children's originality is curbed.

How to change this type of setting? We must make the teachers and the heads of the schools understand that sports gives people the chance to get together and have fun, experience success and achievement, keep fit and healthy and learn physical and technical skills. It helps children to develop timing, balance and coordination, improve their mental skills, co-operate and the ability to communicate with others. It enhances motivation, organisation, leadership and interpersonal skills.

In a developing country like India, teachers in schools when they teach sports, face many constraints like lack of equipments and specially trained physical education teachers. Students and other teachers should understand the fact that sport and physical education can improve people's lives in many ways. Equal importance should be given to sports and academic subjects. The physical education teachers must be trained to handle classes of children with varied aged groups. They must be trained to plan their sessions for different classes with progression giving ample opportunity for challenging tasks. The traditional way of evaluating a physical education teacher, based on the number of children who participated at district, zone and state levels from his/her school, should be detached from the existing norms.

Usage of standard equipments for all classes should be stopped and provision of equipments suitable to the age level should be implemented. We are in need for a new area of athlete development personnel equipped to work specifically with 8-15 year olds drawing together activities aimed at generating team spirit, fun and enjoyment. Such people should be identified as pacesetters according to the importance of their role in the athlete development programme process, clearly differentiating their role as teachers and coaches. They should be open for accepting the fact that there is a lot of difference in dealing with a large group of young children and coaching a squad where small numbers are guided in pursuit of a specific skill. They should understand and accept that for many reasons a talented child at the age of 11 might not be a champion of the future and that they are not in the business of pressuring young children and should encourage all round development.

The aim of the pacesetter should be to develop young people socially and physically through the introduction of athletics in a fun environment and not to produce young individual champions. To get such a trained pacesetter, the existing training methodology in the training colleges must undergo a drastic change. The products of such colleges must suit to the present day needs of the children.

Growth and development of the children play an important role in their physical, intellectual and emotional achievements and accordingly, their implications for sports also differ. It is to be remembered that age is not the only factor while determining which level the child should fit into. Children move through developmental stages of different rates. They need to move through the skills progressions in a planned, sequential manner according to their individual development. The principles of motor learning with reference to the age of the children also should be considered very seriously. At the age of six to 13, the children are supple, and therefore speed and skill could be developed.

The years from seven to 11 are known as the skill hungry years. It is important that skills are taught well right from the outset, as it is virtually impossible to correct some technical faults later. Practice will make perfect but the skills may be perfectly wrong. Early motor learning should be broad, varied and general in nature. This provides sound base for later, more refined, specialised and complex learning. The more numerous and varied the dynamic stereotypes acquired through motor learning, the greater the capacity to learn new skills and modify existing patterns. A rich repertoire of fundamental movement skills, also mean the athlete is less prone to injury.

Teaching the game like football, basketball and hockey, are to be modified into invasions games. The teacher can invent small games that involve the skills of invading other teams area, and this could bring out the team strategy and cooperation. Instead of the teacher telling the children what is to be done, the children should be allowed to think and find out for themselves what they should do. It has a greater value in the later years.

The children could be made into smaller groups and asked to invent their own games. They should tell the teacher the area required for playing, number of players, rules, how points are scored and such other facts. The teacher as a facilitator should provide them with what they want. They will do excellently well better than us. In such invasion games, children learn how to outwit their opponents and score when playing. They develop skills in finding and using space to keep the ball. In all game activities, children think about how to use skills, strategies and tactics to outwit the opposition.

Children will develop and adapt games themselves, making up their own rules and choosing what equipment to use. They will play a wider range of games, with even sides that go end-to-end on larger play fields, improving their accuracy and consistency, and learning new invasion game techniques — how to plan tactics as a team, and how to apply them as a team member. They will learn how to evaluate their own and others' performances, and how to identify a focus for improvement. They will also learn to apply their understanding and skills from net games like volleyball, throw ball, badminton and the like, striking and fielding games cricket and softball, and athletics to new invasion games problems. They will also find how playing games can contribute to good health. While children do this much for themselves, the physical education teacher must be a very good planner of sessions. Good sessions in physical education do not just happen but those sessions require good planning and organisation.

Before planning the activities, it is important to think about the children they are teaching and then plan the sessions according to the needs of the children and levels of experience. Planning helps the teacher and the taught to achieve objectives and ambitions. These objectives may be ones of enjoyment, participation or improving skill.

While setting objectives, utmost care is to be infused lest it can hinder progress. Hence, the objectives must be Specific, Measurable, Agreed, Realistic, Time-framed, Exciting and Recorded (SMARTER). The safety aspect should be taken care of before and after the session by the way of warm-up and cool-down routines in order to reduce the risk of injury.

Children colliding with each other are one of the most common hazards in sport, particularly with large numbers and activities that involve running and chasing. At the end of the session, the teacher should always try to recap on what the groups have achieved. This enhances progress and learning. The children should be insisted upon clearing all the equipments used during the session and neatly arrange them in their places. This would improve the responsibility of the children in taking care of their equipments and play materials.

Children should also be encouraged always to drink plenty of water after the session. After the session, a teacher should evaluate his/her own lesson. This is important because it forms the basis for future planning. It paves way for evaluating our programme as a teacher, as well as giving us a feedback on the progress of our own groups. To help the group's progress in their skills, there needs to be continuity and progress from session to session. When a course or session is ahead, there should be individual session objectives, mid-term objectives and long-term objectives. Those who fail to plan should be prepared to fail.

The equipments the teacher uses in the session add to the variety and challenges to the children. When planning sessions, if the items needed are not at hand, many items could be improvised. For throwing and catching games that do not involve bouncing of the balls, items like paper balls, rag balls, bean bags and cloth balls could be made and used.

The task of making such balls could be given to the children, which they would do excellently and readily well, since they plan and make for their own playtime. For area markers, empty plastic water bottles could be filed with sand and painted in brilliant colours would suffice. Equipment is vital because the sessions run smoothly and children will have sufficient opportunity to improve their skills.

We should remember that we do not always need to have standard equipment, for many games we can use any type of ball. The more equipment we have, the more chances our children have to practice their skills, because it enables them to work in smaller groups, every one getting opportunity to play and have more fun.

As subject and class teachers are appointed with reference to the number of children they have to handle, physical education teachers also must be appointed in relation to the number of children they have to manage. For a minimum of 50 students, there should be at least three physical education teachers so that each group could plan independently their sessions in accordance with the available equipments.

Socioeconomic Factors Affecting Physical Activity

Physical activity is generally defined as any bodily movement produced by skeletal muscles that results in energy expenditure above resting level. The terms exercise and physical fitness are closely related to, but distinct from, physical activity. Exercise is a subset of physical activity defined as: planned, structured, and repetitive bodily movement done to improve or maintain one or more components of physical fitness. Physical fitness is a set of attributes that people have or achieve that relates to the ability to perform physical activity. Thus sport, generally speaking, is seen as a more specialised and organised sector within the much broader concept of physical activity.

The term health-enhancing physical activity is frequently used in relation to the health benefits gained from physical activity. It should be understood as any form of physical activity that benefits health and functional capacity without undue harm or risk. There are a number of ways to categorise physical activity and inactivity related to intensity or expenditure of energy. In order to gain health benefits in a comfortable way, moderate intensity physical activity carried out regularly is most effective for most people. Moderate intensity physical activity is the type of activity that raises the heartbeat and leaves you feeling warm and slightly out of breath. For most people, this is activity equivalent to a brisk walk, and means that the metabolism is raised to at least three times its resting level. Vigorous intensity physical activities are activities like running or fast cycling, if they are fast enough to work up a sweat and get you out of breath. Vigorous intensity activity raises the metabolism to at least six times its resting level. Vigorous intensity activities are usually achieved through sport or exercise.

In most western European countries, the steeply growing demand for mobility over several decades has been satisfied mainly through the increased use of private cars. Similar patterns have been observed in recent years in the eastern part of the Region. European societies have become increasingly carfriendly for a variety of reasons. As a consequence, the role of physically active forms of transport such as cycling and walking has decreased dramatically. In addition, barriers such as the real or perceived level of safety associated with these forms of transport have prevented many people from integrating cycling or walking into their lifestyle.

Another barrier to cycling and walking is the increase in distances travelled because of the geographical separation of living, working, shopping and leisure activities. Physical activity is favoured in neighbourhoods characterised by higher residential density, land use mix, and street connectivity, and more green and open spaces for recreation. In addition, the quality of the neighbourhood environment, especially in terms of aesthetic attributes and perceived safety and security, affects the willingness of residents to make physically active use of their housing environment. Technical developments such as elevators and devices that make household chores less physically demanding have also influenced opportunities for physical activity in the local environment.

Technical developments have been most influential regarding opportunities for physical activity in occupational settings: a large proportion of employees now spend most of their work time sitting with little or no physical activity. This is partly because the service sector has expanded continuously in most countries, at the expense of the agricultural and industrial sectors. The policy and sociocultural environment provided by employers is also an important determinant for the physical activity behaviour of employees. For example, it has been demonstrated that providing a parking space at work has a significant impact on the mode of transport used by employees, favouring motorised transport. Similarly, other company policies such as offering cars as fringe benefits do not encourage physically active mobility.

Children spend more time in institutions than ever before. This alone has probably resulted in less physical activity for them while growing up. Academic demands have also increased, often at the expense of physical education lessons, and despite evidence suggesting that more physical activity could be associated with better academic performance. In addition, many European cities are reporting less cycling and walking in commuting to and from school, especially in cities.

Leisure-time physical activity is subject to changing trends. Organised sports activities have long provided substantial and varied opportunities for activity for many groups. This is still the case, but some indicators suggest that people, especially adults, now give more priority to unorganised forms of activity, such as attending fitness centres or exercising alone or with friends.It seems that leisure-time activity among adults has not changed or declined to the same extent as physical activity in other settings. The real concern is among children and adolescents—not least due to the attractiveness of screen-based activities. As part of efforts to raise levels of physical activity, increased focus should be put on how to reduce sedentary behaviour, in addition to promoting physical activity.

Increasing inequalities within and between countries are now regarded as one of the critical factors that influence health. It is likely that this situation also influences levels of physical activity, as a correlation has been documented between socioeconomic status and activity levels. Surveys have shown that both adults and children from lower socioeconomic groups tend to be active less regularly and more sedentary than those of higher socioeconomic status. The mechanisation of labour has brought a general homogenisation to the levels of work-related physical activity among all social groups; it is therefore more probable that socioeconomic differentials in overall physical activity levels originate from variations in leisure-time physical activity. Lower-income families are also found to participate less in sports for recreation.

Several possible reasons have been suggested to explain why individuals from lower socioeconomic groups tend to be less physically active than those of higher socioeconomic status: they have access to fewer attractive facilities, programmes and other opportunities for physical activity to stimulate an active lifestyle; lower socioeconomic groups are in general less educated and have a lower awareness of and a less positive attitude to the benefits of being physically active; they have less income to pay for these activities; and they report feeling more insecure in their local environment and more worried about crime and a lack of safety in their neighbourhoods compared to higher-income groups.

Our modern way of living has largely eliminated physical activity as one of the fundamental stimuli from our lives. The growth of noncommunicable lifestyle diseases and the epidemic increase in obesity provide clear evidence of this imbalance between our lifestyles and our physical requirements. Physical inactivity is a state of relatively complete physical rest, which does not provide sufficient stimulus for human organs to maintain their normal structures, functions and regulations. Physical inactivity has become a major risk factor for chronic noncommunicable diseases in populations.

Epidemiological research has proven that 15-20% of the overall risk for coronary heart disease, type 2 diabetes, colon cancer, breast cancer and fractured hips in the elderly is attributable to physical inactivity. The overall disease burden in the European Region caused by physical inactivity is estimated to be 3.5%. In The world health report 2002, the proportion of deaths attributable to physical inactivity in the European Region was estimated to be 5-10%.

Based on actual rates of disease and death of physically inactive and active people in the Danish population, a change from inactivity to activity from the age of 30 up to the age of 80, would translate into a gain in life expectancy of between 2.8 and 7.8 years for men and between 4.6 and 7.3 years for women, depending on the degree of activity increase. Another Danish study shows that physically inactive people can expect between 8 and 10 fewer life years without a major disease than physically active people.

Based on epidemiological studies, the economic consequences of physical inactivity have been shown to be substantial on health care costs, but even greater on indirect costs, which include the value of economic output lost because of illness, disease-related work disabilities and premature death. The cost in monetary terms is estimated to be 910 million a year for a population of 10 million where half the population is too inactive to enjoy health benefits from regular physical activity. It is calculated that 3.1million extra days of sick leave each year are attributable to physical inactivity in a population of 5.5 million people.

During the past decade, several assessments of the available scientific evidence have shown the powerful potential of physical activity to benefit health. A recent review states that there is now strong evidence showing that physical activity has beneficial effects on the pathogenesis of all important metabolic syndrome-specific disorders, all important heart and vascular diseases, and osteoporosis. There is also strong or moderate evidence illustrating the positive health effects on the disease-specific symptoms of all these diseases and those of chronic obstructive pulmonary disease, osteoarthritis, fibromyalgia, chronic fatigue syndrome, certain types of cancer and depression.

Additionally, in virtually all disease states, there exists strong or moderate evidence to show that physical activity improves functional capacity and quality of life. Mortality rates from noncommunicable diseases increase with high body weights and are markedly increased at levels designated as obese. Regular physical activity is a protective factor against unhealthy weight gains. The role of physical activity in the management of overweight and obesity is threefold: 1) prevention of weight gain; 2) prevention of health consequences of obesity; and 3) weight reduction. From the public health perspective, areas 1 and 2 are the most important.

Having the opportunity to enjoy quality recreation is vital to the health and personal development of all individuals, regardless of gender, functional ability, ethnocultural background, age or socioeconomic status. Children and young people are a particular concern, especially those living in low-income families. Although all children and young people have the right to engage in play and recreation activities, there are clear indications that their level of participation in recreation, sport and physical activity is often inversely proportional to their family's income level. Barriers affecting the participation of many individuals include user costs and user fees, awareness of opportunities, transportation, cultural and language barriers, and access to local recreation facilities and safe places to play. Keys to overcoming these barriers include:

— policies that provide low-cost or free access to public recreation facilities for low-income families and others in need;

— subsidised programmes to teach motor, sport and physical activity skills that encourage lifelong participation;

— the provision of indoor and outdoor recreation facilities, especially within low-income neighbourhoods;

— the provision of indoor and outdoor facilities that are physically accessible and support active lifestyles for people with disabilities;

— sensitivity to cultural differences in programmes and facilities; and

— coordinated communication approaches to alleviate barriers to awareness about such opportunities.

Based on physiological, epidemiological, and clinical evidence, international experts agree that, to produce substantial health benefits, the adequate level of physical activity for adults can be expressed as follows: Every adult should accumulate 30 minutes or more of moderate-intensity physical activity on most, preferably all, days of the week. Moderate-intensity physical activity corresponds to quick or brisk walking. Cycling, swimming and gardening with moderate effort are other modes of moderate-intensity physical activity.

The recommended duration of 30 minutes can be split up into shorter periods, ideally no less than 10 minutes, but even shorter bouts contribute to substantial health benefits. A good example of this is using stairs instead of elevators. Adults who do not meet the recommended level of activity should increase their participation in different ways. Those who do not engage in regular physical activity should begin by incorporating a few minutes of increased activity into their day, building up gradually to 30 minutes per day. Those who are active on an irregular basis should strive to adopt a more consistent activity pattern.

To improve or to specialise in different forms of fitness, a selection of various types of fitness-adapted activities are needed. If such more or less specialised and repeated activities are added to the basic recommended amount of moderate-intensity physical activity, improvements in both fitness and health will be achieved. All movement contributes to energy expenditure and is important for weight management. However, it is likely that for many people, 45-60 minutes of moderate-intensity physical activity per day is necessary to prevent weight gain or reduce overweight. This figure is influenced by individual metabolic rate, food intake and type of diet.

The recommendations for adults are also appropriate for older adults. Older people should take particular care to keep moving and retain their mobility and their lean body mass through daily activity. Additionally, specific activities that promote improved strength, coordination and balance are particularly beneficial for older people.

Current physical activity recommendations for children and young people are: All young people should participate in physical activity of at least moderate intensity for 60 minutes per day. At least twice a week some of these activities should help to enhance and maintain muscular strength, flexibility, and bone health. The activity may be divided into shorter periods throughout the day, and should be as versatile and inspiring as possible. A recent study suggested that physical activity levels in children should be about 30 minutes higher than the current international guidelines of at least 60 minutes per day of physical activity of at least moderate intensity, to prevent clustering of cardiovascular disease risk factors. Another important issue concerning childhood health is weight control. Regular physical activity can help prevent and reduce obesity or maintain a healthy weight.

Comprehensive Approach to Physical Activity

A large number of causes underlie the current low levels of physical activity. All evidence to date demonstrates the need for a broad range of instruments and actors to curb or reverse the trend. This corresponds to what has been found in other areas of public health work, where determined populationbased efforts following continuous and comprehensive approaches have to be used. The work must be supported by authorities and stakeholders at all levels. Cooperating networks, alliances and partnerships have to be established to achieve synergy and complementarity. The leading countries in this area are more and more often referring to such a comprehensive or "ecological" approach as the foundation for plans and action. According to this approach, the elements for success are:

- adopting an integrated, multidisciplinary and comprehensive approach
- including a complementary range of actions

— working at the individual, community, environmental and policy levels.

An ecological approach aims both at facilitating healthy lifestyles for individuals and influencing policies to ensure that they create the framework for action and encourage the necessary social and cultural changes. Strategies can be categorised, based on their focus, according to the following interconnected ecological levels:

— intrapersonal factors;

— interpersonal processes;

— institutional or organisational factors;

— community factors; and

— public policy.

Until now much, perhaps too much, of the effort in health promotion work has been concentrated on the responsibility of individuals. Reviews of the determinants of obesity reveal that any attempt to achieve behavioural change needs to consider social and cultural, as well as physical environments. It is obvious that overweight and obesity are not only an individual concern. This health problem and its determinants must be given a much broader focus and must be addressed by facilitating access to healthy food and physical activity in combined and complementary ways. Other health issues such as tobacco, seatbelts, breastfeeding and recycling have succeeded in generating social change at levels similar to those necessary to address the decreasing levels of physical activity and the associated obesity epidemic. These successful models have predominantly targeted environmental and population policy; such a social-change approach should also be applicable to physical activity promotion. It is crucially important to have political support for population-based change strategies.

Ensuring regulations where possible, adequate funding, intersectoral commitments and integrated strategies within existing and new programmes and structures requires political involvement. The health sector has a leading role in creating this foundation.

For most of the development of mankind, physical activity has been an essential part of life for virtually everyone. Physical activity was not a choice but a necessity. In the past few decades, rapid changes in transport, communication, urban planning, architecture and leisure possibilities have made physical activity one choice among many. At the same time, sport for all has developed in many European countries and has become a new choice available to many people.

The greater range of choices could theoretically have led to an overall more physically active society. Unfortunately, this has not proved to be the case. While participation in leisure activities and sports has increased in some subgroups, declines have been observed in physical activity in everyday life in many countries such as Finland and Switzerland. The fact that differences in physical activity behaviour are found not only between individuals but also between population groups, shows that this choice is not only an individual one. It also explains the limitations of physical activity promotion that targets only individual behaviour, as well as isolated communication approaches. The often-cited "lack of time" as a barrier to physical activity can be an indicator of both the low priority this issue has for many people but also of a real problem of fitting activities into a busy day. It is necessary to disseminate information about the benefits and possibilities of physical activity and to encourage people to be physically active. Yet this alone will not create change at the general population level unless there is adequate provision in terms of infrastructure and safety, and a context in which physical activity is the norm and social support is provided where needed. There is an abundance of examples of good practice from different countries, including sporting events such as runs throughout Europe, pedestrian zones in many of our cities, cycling networks in Denmark and the Netherlands, and traffic interventions like the London congestion charge.

Increasing the Levels of Physical Activity

The importance of physical activity as a health determinant is a relatively new part of health science. Consequently, trials conducted to increase people's activity levels have a relatively short history. Knowledge gaps in this area still exist, but an important and promising fact is that we already have sufficient knowledge and experience to provide a framework for successful action. Further, there is moderate evidence that activity is stimulated by urban design features such as density, street connectivity and mixed land use, and by perceived and objectively-determined environmental attributes such as aesthetics, convenience (pavements), access (green spaces), safety and security. For those interventions listed where cost-benefit analysis has been conducted, all are shown to be highly cost-effective (active transport, comprehensive worksite approaches, individually-adapted health behaviour change, and creation of and/or enhanced access to places for physical activity combined with informational outreach activities).

It is important to note that many of the studies included in these reviews lasted no longer than a year, thus making it difficult to assess the long-term effects of the interventions. Further long-term studies are needed to assess these effects. Other interventions not found to be sufficiently effective individually may have greater effect in combined, comprehensive approaches.

The choice of interventions and measures should also take into account local resources, characteristics and target groups. Further efforts to develop the next generation of preventive interventions must focus on building relationships with communities and deriving interventions from the communities' assessments of their needs and priorities. Models should be developed that encourage members of the community and researchers to work together to design, train for and conduct such programmes.

A healthier and more productive population is a higher goal for national health policy in every nation. With the increase in lifestyle-related health problems, a paradigm shift must take place in national understanding of the health policies needed to reach this goal. Health care and health promotion must be seen and practised as complementary parts of health policy as a whole. The importance of integrating the health promotion element into future national health work should be indicated through organising, policymaking and the use of resources.

As one of the main lifestyle-related health determinants, physical activity must be included as an important part of the intersectoral public health work of national governments. Developing understanding and commitments from other sectors as to their roles and ways of cooperating, is one of the crucial prerequisites for achieving success.

Health ministries need to take the lead in developing national policies with clear vision, strategies, action plans and programmes. Specific goals, a division of responsibilities, baseline reports and effective independent monitoring and evaluation of output and outcomes are vital. The ministry responsible for health has to show leadership, driving as well as facilitating effective collaboration with other ministries, based on their areas of responsibility and focusing on the multiple benefits of encouraging more physical activity.

To create the necessary awareness and attention at regional and local levels to facilitate healthy lifestyle choices as easy local choices, a determined and supportive national leadership is crucial. Strategies defining how to collaborate and build capacity at regional and local levels should be an important part of national policy and action. A key factor in the establishment of regional and local policies is the provision of financial resources, including from the national government.

The most appropriate actor in creating both public and intersectoral political awareness and action for this comprehensive approach is the ministry of health. By establishing interministerial collaboration, a complementary, committed and integrated framework for action can be achieved.

If physical activity is to be practised regularly, it has to be integrated into people's daily lives, their daily settings such as workplaces and schools, their way to and from work and school, their homes and their leisure time. As emphasised earlier, the healthy choices must be the natural, easy and regular choices, most of which will be at local level. It is mainly local communities who can provide regular and easily available daily opportunities for physical activity. Establishing local leadership, understanding and capacity is a crucial factor for achieving success. Local awareness, local willingness and local action are therefore essential in creating the social and physical environments necessary to motivate individuals sufficiently to be physical active. If local governments and communities are given political, technical and economic support from national and regional authorities, they will be in a position to achieve wider reaching goals.

It is therefore absolutely essential to recognise the key role of local governments and to make use of and activate local resources. Local awareness and knowledge in this area will stimulate willingness to act. This awareness and knowledge must be cultivated in appropriate and motivating ways. Further, local work on physical activity must be rooted in a sustainable and future-oriented framework of political involvement and commitments, plans, interdepartmental and intersectoral collaboration that is supported with sufficient financial and human resources. The overall goal of creating the opportunity for all groups to engage in physical activity must be reflected in all parts of this framework.

Local plans of action and choices of new interventions should be based in part on interventions with a proven ability to increase levels of activity. Local goals, characteristics and resources should also be taken into account. There is a growing body of evidence with many good practical examples of how to mobilise at the local level, which interventions should be given priority, and how they should be implemented. There is also a range of examples of how to facilitate physical activity for different groups in different settings. This experience and these good examples should be systematised and adapted to specific national and local conditions.

National and regional authorities usually have the most ambitious statements for public health work. They also have a vested economic interest in encouraging healthy living. Offering local authorities technical and economic support is one way of enhancing the credibility of national and regional authorities' public health work in this area.

The Bangkok Charter for Health Promotion in a Globalised World emphasises that the health sector has a key leadership role to play in building policies and partnerships for health promotion. The promotion of physical activity provides an ideal opportunity to do this. Ensuring that there is a comprehensive and intersectoral approach to achieving higher levels of health-enhancing physical activity requires convincing and committed leadership. The health sector has the mandate to take this lead. At national, regional and local levels, it should invite and motivate different sectors and stakeholders to collaborate in promoting physical activity. Health authorities are aware of and able to convey most of the key messages about the need for common efforts to give greater priority to this health area.

Health professionals have more or less regular individual contact with a considerable part of the population. This contact must be used to inform and educate their clients about the causes of disease and reduced health, especially with regard to preventable lifestyle-related diseases. It can also assist in answering the important question of what individuals can do personally to reduce the causes of ill health. Health professionals represent figures of authority to most people, especially the elderly, and this authority should be better utilised in promoting healthier lifestyles, including physical activity. Primary care is an extremely important setting for the promotion of physical activity. Advice and prescribed medicines from physicians are seen by many as the ultimate source of and resource for healthier lives.

Physical activity must be a part of this, in the form of opportunistic advice or encouragement, as well as more profound and committing written "prescriptions". Such written recommendations, often named "active prescriptions" or "exercise on prescription", are shown to achieve a better response from patients than solely verbal advice; they have been introduced in several countries on a larger or smaller scale. In addition to written recommendations, it has been found that good results are achieved where the patients set their own goals, where recommended activities are individually adapted, and where individuals are followed up with qualified support after consultation with a health professional.

It has also been suggested that introducing "exercise on prescription" programmes will increase general awareness, raise the status of physical activity in society and facilitate recognition among all health professionals of the fact that it can be used as both prevention and treatment for diseases. One challenge in using the health sector to proactively promote physical activity in such a way is the need to provide physicians and practitioner nurses with better education, practical experience and more knowledge about why and how to use physical activity.

As an employer and generator of journeys, the health sector has a major potential influence on physical activity, and a responsibility to set an example of best practice to other sectors by offering certain groups of patients and staff the opportunity to be physically active within and around the health care system.

Physical Activity in Schools

Time given to physical education at both the primary and secondary school levels has fallen on average over the last decade. Greater priority is given to important theoretical disciplines such as mathematics and language. Increasing pressure for academic time may also lead to a decrease in time for unstructured physical activity during playtimes and lunch breaks. At the same time, many countries are reporting less cycling and walking to and from school, mostly explained by the real or perceived danger of traffic. Computers and cafeterias and greater freedom to use indoors facilities have also contributed to schooldays with lower levels of physical activity.

A number of projects have shown that test results in core academic subjects do not decline where physical education lessons are increased at the expense of lessons in these core subjects. These projects do, however, lead to an improvement in the children's health. Many studies also give strong indications of a significant positive relationship between physical activity and cognitive functioning in children and adolescents. Some evidence has also been found linking levels of physical activity and children's ability to concentrate in class. If schools and kindergartens are going to compensate for the increased sedentary life of children, the best way of doing this is probably offering a variety of physical activities. In addition to improving the physical education led by qualified teachers, such an approach must also consider encouraging more unorganised activity during breaks and other periods of unorganised time at school, the use of outdoor environments in teaching different subjects, short classroom-based physical activities either at the beginning of or during lessons, and the use of walking and cycling to and from home. More physical activity at school could be an important tool in combating the increasing obesity epidemic and improving the overall health of children.

Physical Activity in Workplaces

As companies try to do more with fewer staff, time constraints and fatigue are becoming part of the job description for the remaining employees. Long hours and lack of rest are a reality. Fortunately, many workplaces do not let the problems degenerate into unmanageable situations. Effective solutions do exist. Regular physical activity, preferably three times a week at moderate or high intensity levels and ideally designed relative to the job and individual capacity, has a positive effect on sick leave. Furthermore, physical activity enhances mood and performance and improves concentration. The evidence base is strong, even if there is a need for more randomised controlled trials of high methodological quality.

Workplaces that encourage regular physical activity report not only improved employee health and fitness, but also increased productivity and morale, reduced injury rates, better employee relations, improved job satisfaction and team spirit. Because most adults spend half their waking hours at work, finding ways to include physical activity during the workday, as well as in transportation to and from the workplace and home, is the most practical way for many adults to become more active.

Outdoor Physical Activities

Compared to other areas of life, leisure has better maintained its capacity to encourage physical activity even if the forms of activity have changed and are still changing. Shorter working hours and more technically-developed lifestyles have given most people more leisure time than in the past. Together with the general increase in mobility, this provides a good basis for practising more physical activity during leisure time.

Sports organisations form the context for physically active leisure for many people. Trends in participation in sports vary between countries in Europe, but the general tendency is towards a stabilisation in the number of members of traditional sports clubs. People who take an active part in sports are much more likely to meet the recommendations for physical activity related to health benefits than those who are not active. Among children, in particular, sports still hold a great appeal in terms of exercise, competitions and the increasing number of activities offered. However, the loss of large numbers of active members during their teenage years is a challenge for sports organisations. Among adults, there is in many countries a "leakage" from organised sports activities to more individual activities, where people exercise either alone or in fitness centres or health studios that are often situated in residential areas, have flexible opening hours and attractive facilities, and meet the requirements of the individual. Another reason may be that more people consider physical exercise as a way of staying fit and healthy. The increasing individualisation of society is also reflected here, and traditional sports organisations need to take this into account if they want to become more attractive and adapt what they offer to more "modern" requirements.

The impressive and valuable voluntary work of sports and outdoor recreation organisations needs more support and encouragement. These organisations should also be motivated and stimulated to broaden their activities in order to retain members with shifting interests and to gain new groups of members. An excellent example of new areas more adapted to individual qualifications is the growing number of clubs promoting and facilitating Nordic walking—walking with use of poles.

Regardless of the preferred form of activity, if it is to be engaged in regularly, it is crucial that access should be good, in terms both of distance and of other attributes like capacity, user groups, attractiveness and cost. Sports activities need sports facilities. Even if most sports facilities, built for more or less specialised activities and used by the fitter and more active part of the population, are theoretically available to everyone, it is clear that they are not attractive to people who are less active. It is still the case in most countries that specialised and expensive sports facilities are given priority in the allocation of economic resources intended to increase and promote physical activity in general.

In our growing awareness of the need to raise levels of physical activity, especially among less active groups, it now seems necessary to achieve a better balance in planning and investing in (local) infrastructure for promoting low threshold unorganised physical activity and recreational sports versus more specialised organised sport. More resources have to be used to provide the less active groups with adapted and appropriate infrastructure. Good examples of this are parks and open areas that encourage active play and various unorganised activities and recreational sports (e.g. many different ball games), pathways and trails, cycle lanes and community recreation centres. Ensuring that such facilities are of good quality and easily accessible is an effective way of raising levels of physical activity.

There is great potential for including more physical activity into our leisure time. The competition from an increasing range of alternative and mostly sedentary leisure pursuits has resulted in a paradoxical claimed "lack of time" for participation in physical activity and sport. The hours that people spend watching television each day are one of the main reason for this "lack of time", and this illustrates the scale of the challenge of informing people and making them aware that physical activity is an instrument that can enrich our lives with fun, self-confidence, energy and health.

Promotion of Physical Activity

Traditionally, the promotion of physical activity has been seen as a job for the leisure and education sectors through the promotion of sport among the general population and within schools, colleges and universities. But in recent years there has been growing recognition that organised sport, while a vital part of the picture, makes a relatively small contribution to levels of physical activity among the general population—less than 10% of the total in many countries. Wider lifestyle activities such as walking and cycling have a major part to play in raising activity levels, and the health sector is increasingly recognising the importance of supporting physical activity for health. The moves towards healthpromoting schools and workplaces are important examples of this, with real potential to improve people's lives and tackle problems such as obesity.

Education, working life, transport and the built environment are at the heart of this approach. If it is to be truly successful, urban planners, transport planners, traffic engineers and architects need to work together with representatives from schools, the leisure and sports sectors, and the health sector. Many of the initiatives that encourage lifestyle physical activity such as safe routes to school, active travel, neighbourhood walkability, attractive green spaces and enhanced building design can also have a positive impact on the environment and sustainability.

Mandating public bodies to work towards common goals is achievable, for example, by creating targets for tackling problems such as childhood obesity that are shared with the transport sector, as well as with education, sport and leisure. Influencing the nongovernmental and commercial sectors requires a different set of approaches. Local networks and alliances, with shared priorities and true commitments to achieving success together, are important for engaging these sectors. The public sector can shape the way in which commercial sector decisions are made, both by influencing the regulatory framework and by promoting an environment in which consumers are able and willing to make healthier choices.

The great challenge for public health lies in reconciling and integrating the different and sometimes competing approaches and interests involved. Improving the opportunities for physical activity requires 'horizontal', cross-cutting approaches, integrating the activities of different sectors at all levels and encouraging them to work together in the face of different organisational structures, priorities and goals. Recognition should also be given to the importance of 'vertical' structures within sectors that place local decision-making in the context of national and regional policies for that sector. The governmental health sector at all levels should accept and take on a convincing leadership role in building networks and alliances and in coordinating action that supports physical activity.

One of the crucial aspects of developing and coordinating a comprehensive plan of public health action is the setting of clear aims, objectives and indicators, against which the success of the work can be monitored. Setting objectives and indicators for a project ensures that it is clear what you are setting out to do, and the mechanisms by which you hope to do it. The process of agreeing on objectives and indicators means that all major stakeholders in a project can be involved at the critical planning phase.

The objectives of a project set out what the project hopes to achieve. Ideally, these should be specific, measurable, achievable, realistic and time-bound ('SMART'). For example, an objective to ensure that all local authorities have published a stated commitment to increasing cycling within their local transportation plans by year ... (a defined year) would be preferable to an objective 'to encourage local authorities to promote cycling'.

Indicators are measured variables, which help to evaluate changes that can be diiectly (and indirectly) related to goals, objectives and targets. They are indirect or partial measures of a ccmplex situation but, if measured sequentially over time, they can indicate the direction and speed of change and serve to compare different areas or groups of people at the same moment in time. Agreeing on a core set of indicators for a project allows stakeholders to focus on the precise element that they are trying to change. For example, a core indicator of 'the proportion of school children walking or cycling to school daily' would direct programme activity specifically towards action on school travel.

Physical Exercise and Weight Loss

Hypertensive patients are routinely advised by their physicians that losing weight and exercising regularly are good for their blood pressure, but relatively few studies have looked to see how effective this combination really is. A study from Duke University recruited 133 sedentary and overweight men and women with mild hypertension to be randomly allocated to one of three groups. The first was a Control group, who had no intervention; the second was an Exercise Only group, who exercised three or four times a week for 45 minutes (jogging and bicycling); and the third was a Combined Treatment group, who in addition to the exercise, took part in weekly group sessions for instruction on weight loss. Each treatment lasted for six months.

Blood pressure was measured both in the clinic and by 24-hour ambulatory monitoring at the beginning and end of the study. The average blood pressure for the whole group of patients at the start of the study was 141/93 mmHg, and the average body weight 202 pounds (a body mass index of 32.5). The participants in the Combined Treatment group lost 7.8 kilograms (17 pounds), compared to 1.8 (4 pounds) in the Exercise Only group, and 0.7 (1.5 pounds) in the Control group. Clinic blood pressure fell by 7.4/5.6 mmHg (systolic/diastolic) in the Combined Treatment group, by 4.4/4.3 mmHg in the Exercise Only group, and 0.9/1.4 mmHg in the

Control group. Similar changes were seen in the ambulatory blood pressure measurements. Blood glucose levels were also reduced in the Combined Treatment group.

The results of this study confirm that the combination of an exercise program with a weight loss program is more effective than exercise alone for lowering blood pressure. Thus exercise on its own lowered the blood pressure by about 4 mmHg and the combination with weight loss by 7 mmHg. While these changes may not seem very big, for people with borderline hypertension they may be all that is needed to avoid needing blood pressure medications. There is also evidence that exercise and weight loss both help to prevent diabetes, which overweight people are particularly prone to and which can have devastating effects in combination with hypertension.

It is well established that people who exercise regularly are at reduced risk of having a heart attack, but it is less certain whether it also protects against strokes. The questions about physical activity asked them about walking, running, bicycling, aerobics, tennis, etc., and also how vigorously they did these various activities. During eight years of follow-up, there were 407 strokes, and it was found that the women who were more physically active were at lower risk. This was still true even after allowing for the facts that they were thinner, less likely to smoke, and ate better diets than the less active women. The lowest risk was in the most active women, whose average weekly activity was equivalent to 20 hours of walking, and whose risk was about half the risk of the inactive women. Strokes can have different causes, the commonest being ischemic strokes, and the next most common hemorrhagic strokes (from a burst artery). The protective effect of exercise was greater for the ischemic type of stroke.

Resistance Exercise Training

The traditional recommendation for exercise programs in people with hypertension is to do aerobic exercise for 30 to 45 minutes on at least three days a week. The effects of resistance (isometric) exercise on resting blood pressure have not been extensively investigated. The analysis described here examined the medical literature for studies in which the effects of a resistance exercise program on resting blood pressure were examined, by comparing the changes in an exercise group with a sedentary control group. Eleven such studies were found, most of which were carried out in people with normal blood pressure.

The average length of training was 14 weeks, with three sessions of 40 minutes a week. The participants performed an average of 10 different muscle-strengthening exercises, with about 20 repetitions of each exercise. The main finding of the analysis was that the average blood pressure decrease in the exercise groups was 3/3 (systolic/diastolic) mmHg more than the changes in the control group. Heart rate was not affected. Body weight did not change, but there was a decrease of body fat, which was matched by an increase of lean body mass.

This analysis suggests that resistance exercise (muscle strengthening) training—sometimes known as circuit training—has a small but beneficial effect on the resting blood pressure. The studies did not include enough people with high blood pressure to be able to say whether the changes would be the same in them, but they would probably be at least as large. Sustained muscle contraction can produce a very large increase of both systolic and diastolic pressure, but the types of exercise described in these studies usually involved repetitions of relatively short duration, which should not be of concern. The bottom line is that while resistance exercise appears to be beneficial for blood pressure, aerobic exercise is still preferable for people with hypertension, in whom weight control is often a factor.

Aerobic exercise is superior as a means of losing weight. Both types of exercise are good for preventing osteoporosis. Aerobic exercise is better for reducing blood pressure, although resistance training may lower diastolic pressure a little. Aerobic exercise lowers the resting heart rate, while resistance exercise has no effect. There is a big increase of both systolic and diastolic pressure during resistance exercise; however, this increase is less when the muscle is trained.

Both types of exercise produce a slight improvement in the blood lipid profile, with a reduction of LDL and an increase of HDL cholesterol. Another beneficial affect is an improvement in insulin sensitivity. Low insulin sensitivity (otherwise known as insulin resistance) is one of the causes of adult onset diabetes. The recommendation is to do 8 to 10 repetitions of a variety of exercises, which include chest press, shoulder press, triceps extension, biceps curl, leg curls, etc. The exercises should be performed two or three times week for about 30 minutes in total at each session.

Exercise is generally recommended for people with hypertension, and one study of Harvard University graduates showed that men who continued a vigorous exercise program were less likely to develop hypertension than those with a sedentary lifestyle. Less vigorous exercise, such as walking, has been found to be associated with a number of health benefits, but no reports have assessed whether it can delay the onset of hypertension. Now a study of Japanese men employed by a gas company in Japan has confirmed that it can. It involved more than 6,000 men who were followed for about ten years.

They had a medical examination every two years, which included an assessment of how they got to work, their leisure time physical activity, their blood pressure, and other health-related factors. More than 600 men became hypertensive during the ensuing 10 years. The main finding was that men whose walk to work took more than 10 minutes had a lower risk of developing hypertension in comparison with those whose walking time was less than 10 minutes. For those whose walking time was more than 20 minutes each way, the risk of hypertension was reduced by 30%. This was independent of other factors such as obesity and leisure time physical activity. However, leisure time physical activity was also associated with less hypertension.

One of the factors that made this study feasible is that employees in Japan typically stay in the same job for many years, so that the way they get to work is unlikely to change very much. The effects of walking were separate from the effects of leisure time physical activity, and also from the effects of exercise on body weight.

The benefits of aerobic exercise are well established, but the effects of muscular-strength training (weight lifting) are less understood. Strength training involves sudden and sustained contraction of muscles against resistance and causes a dramatic increase of both systolic and diastolic pressure, which in the long run can cause thickening of the heart muscle. These effects are thought to be unhealthy from a cardiovascular point of view. Aerobic exercise enlarges the chamber of the heart, but does not make the muscle thicker, and it also makes the arteries less stiff. These changes are thought to be beneficial. An Australian study compared 19 young weight lifters (average age 26) with 19 healthy sedentary subjects. The weightlifters did at least 3 sessions per week to build their muscle strength, but did not do regular aerobic exercise.

A number of measurements were made, which included blood pressure, muscle strength (measured by a handgrip test), aerobic fitness (maximum oxygen consumption), heart size (by echocardiography), and arterial stiffness (measured from the pressure and flow waveform recorded noninvasively from the arteries). The weightlifters were slightly shorter, but weighed more than the sedentary subjects, and had a greater grip strength, but their aerobic fitness was the same. Their systolic pressure was higher and their diastolic lower than the sedentary subjects (120/59 versus 109/63 mmHg). Their pulse pressure was thus also greater (60 versus 50 mmHg). The weight lifters had larger hearts, but not when allowance was made for their greater body size. Their arteries were about 25% stiffer than the arteries of the sedentary subjects.

The conventional recommendation for exercise is that it should be done for at least 30 minutes a day for five days a week to get the maximum cardiovascular benefit. But for many people, finding a 30-minute block of time during the day is difficult, and many people simple don't enjoy exercising for that length of time. A study of 32 sedentary adults randomly allocated them to one of three groups. For each group, the goal was to get a total of 30 minutes of walking on six days a week. One group did a single 30-minute bout each day, one did three 10-minute bouts and the third chose the duration of each bout, as long as they were for at least five minutes.

Participants met with a counselor for 15-30 minutes once a week and were given goals to achieve, which involved gradually increasing the amount of walking over several weeks. Over an eight-month period, all three groups gradually increased the duration of walking to the goal level of 180 minutes a week. Both blood pressure and body fat were decreased, and the changes in all three groups were about the same. When the participants were asked what skills were most useful in maintaining their walking habits, there were six that ranked highly.

Although the general benefits of regular exercise are well established, it has not been clearly shown that people who have hypertension get the same protection from heart disease as others. A Swedish survey of 642 men, all aged 55, was begun in 1970 and then they were followed for the next 25 years. They were asked about their lifestyles at the start of the study, including their exercise habits. They were divided into two groups: 'non-vigorous' exercise (men whose most vigorous activity was something like walking to work), and 'vigorous' exercise (men who did things like running, swimming, or playing tennis for at least four hours a week). About one third of the men were hypertensive, and those of them who reported vigorous exercise had one third the risk of dying from heart disease compared with the more sedentary men over the following 25 years. And their death rate from any cause was cut by more than half. The benefits of exercise were greater in the men with hypertension than in the others who had normal blood pressure. Many people with hypertension are worried that exercise may be dangerous, because it raises the blood pressure. If the pressure is really high, exercise is not recommended until it is under control, but it doesn't have to be normal. In the hypertensive men who exercised vigorously in this study, the average pressure was 157/97 mm Hg. One of the most interesting findings was that vigorous exercise appeared to be more beneficial in the hypertensive men than in the others.

3

Quality Health Education

Policy and practice in school evolve slowly and unevenly. Current practice in school systems, and even in individual schools, invariably reflects different layers of historical influence overlapping each other like tiles upon a roof. The oldest influence derives from policies and practices dating from colonial times when personal community hygiene was at the heart of health programmes. Indeed the subject was then referred to as 'hygiene' in all the three countries under study. In India, this emphasis was further reinforced by Gandhi's view of Basic Education based on an idealised and self-sufficient village economy. The attainment of independence in India was not followed by attempts to render their school curricula more relevant to the needs of the majority of children who lived and might continue to live in rural areas. That had been the policy of colonial governments who wished to maintain distance and separation between ruling and indigenous communities. Whilst it was also the message of Gandhi, it was not welcome in countries determined to take their place in an international economy or to citizens whose ambition was for their children to move outwards and upwards, make money and gain power rather than remaining in rural areas.

In India during the 1960s the effect of the 'curriculum revolution' in the United States was felt directly through the influence of returning scholars. This had both positive and negative impacts on the future of health education programmes. On the one hand, emphasis on subject-based curriculum development geared to the development of cognitive skills was institutionalised by the creation of specialist curriculum centres, themselves organised on subject lines, with specialist panels competing for available school time. There was no place for health as a subject and no interest in it at first as a cross-curricular theme. If health education figured at all it was only when personnel from the health sector came to visit schools.

The school health education division promotes health education in the school system of education in the country. It has developed & revised curricula from primary to higher secondary level including health education materials. It coordinates with National Council of Educational Research and Training (NCERT) & Central Board of Secondary Education (CBSE) for inclusion of health education subjects in formal and non formal education. Most of the states in India have state health education bureaus that are patterned after the Central Health Education Bureau. Besides, the Central and State Health Education Bureaus there is also the Family Welfare Training and Research Centre (FWTRC), in Mumbai that was established in 1957 as the first Family Planning Training Centre. It has the responsibility for the training needs of state and district level categories of health personnel from the Western zone. The centre also conducts a one year postgraduate diploma in health education (DHE).

Another health education institution is the Gandhigram Institute of Rural Health and Family Welfare Trust (GIRHFWT), Gandhigram, Tamil Nadu. The Gandhigram institution is also functioning as one of the Central Training Institutions in India to provide training to functionaries of Health and Family Welfare of Kerala, Karnataka, Pondicherry, Andaman & Nicobar Islands as well as Tamil Nadu. The institute also conducts regular diploma in health education (DHE) of one year. Another such institution is the All India Institute of Hygiene and Public Health (AIIH&PH), Calcutta that was established in 1932 with the assistance of Rockefeller Foundation.

The apex institution for health education in the nongovernmental sector in India is Voluntary Health Association of India (VHAI) that was established in 1970. It is a not-for-profit federation of 24 State Voluntary Health Associations (VHA) that links more than 4,000 health care institutions and grassroots level community health programmes spread across the country. The organisation has a State VHA unit, communications unit that publishes health education materials, community health and development unit that conducts training programmes, information unit that maintains health, development, and family welfare related information, and women's health and drugs unit that deals with these two issues.

One of the strengths of the health education in India is an elaborate multi tier infrastructure of functionaries in the government and nongovernmental sector. In the governmental sector the Central Health Education Bureau and its network with State Health Education Bureaus that link the districts blocks, and communities is quite praiseworthy. In the nongovernmental sector also the Voluntary Health Association of India and its network with State Voluntary Health Associations that link grassroots organisations is commendable. Most health educators were either graduates or post graduates with more than two thirds having been trained in health education. While there is no degree offered with a major in health education, yet there are many well qualified health educators. Another strength of the health education in India is its strong emphasis on information dissemination. India is a vast country with 15 official languages and several hundred dialects. In this backdrop it is very difficult to reach the masses and despite this challenge the health education campaigns have been informing the public regarding health and family planning messages.

One of the settings for health education is in schools. In India, several health education programmes for children have been designed including incorporation of health education in curricula. An innovative approach has also been implemented-the child to child programme-where children actually educate each other about health. School health education programmes have been among strengths of health education in India. A search of recent health education articles indexed in CINAHL and MEDLINE revealed that knowledge, attitude, practice surveys are very common Though most of these are not theory based and are relatively few given the magnitude of health and family planning problems in the country even then this is indicative that there are systematic attempts at accomplishing needs assessment function of health education.

Most of the current health education interventions are knowledge based interventions. Further, to the best of our knowledge we could find only a solitary intervention that used community diagnosis and participation in planning the intervention and another one that used information, motivation and behavioural skills model in designing the intervention. Otherwise most of the interventions were a theoretical. Finally, to the best of our knowledge we could find only a solitary policy intervention that worked on school policy to influence tobacco use. It is well known that knowledge is necessary but not sufficient for behaviour change.

There is a definitive need for more robust theory-based health education interventions for behaviour change and more health promotion interventions that influence policies and organisational constructs. Most of the campaigns of information dissemination in the government sector as well as the nongovernmental sector use newspapers, posters, and pamphlets. Almost 40% percent of the Indian population is illiterate and use of print media to impart health messages is controversial. Further, 60% of promotions do not exhibit adequate information. Mass media campaigns have not been successful in reaching rural populations living in far flung and vulnerable areas. Only one fifth of health education functionaries in the government sector were placed at the rural level while three fourths of the population is rural. This lop sided allocation of resources is a weakness of the health education in India.

Another weakness of health education in India is that despite having a large work force of functionaries that perform health education there is no quality assurance. The system of continuing education is largely non existent. There are no avenues for promotion of health education functionaries. The profession is largely disorganised with no association or holding of annual meetings. Weakness of postgraduate medical and health education in India. They observe that training is in apprenticeship style format rather than appraisal style format and selection of assessment tools is not guided by modern educational theory.

India has a rich cultural heritage and in reaching rural populations folk media provide an effective means. Most suitable for working with tribal populations appear to be the media of the spoken work, song and drama, games, exhibitions at the weekly market and yearly festivals, and pictorial aids. There is need to tap into the potential of folk media in health education. Health educators have not yet tapped perhaps the greatest resources such as religious leaders, traditional healers, and traditional birth attendants (dais). India is a pluralistic society and there are a vast numb er of community resources that can be harnessed for health education. There is a need to enhance the involvement of many of these functionaries in health education.

Patient education is in its infancy stages in India. Ill people and family members in a hospital are a captive audience and tend to be receptive to public health messages. Further health workers at clinics and during home visits can inform clients about health. The setting of worksite based health education is non existent in India and needs to be developed more.

The World Health Organisation has introduced the Communication for Behavioural Impact (COMBI) approach based on social marketing principles to the prevention of lymphatic filariasis in India. There are plans to extend this approach for achieving behavioural impact in combating HIV/AIDS, tuberculosis, and malaria. There is need for more theoretically robust health education interventions. Some medical colleges have initiated systematic training and application of health education by physicians.

The training covers the modes of disease transmission, the role of nutrition, environmental health, first aid, lifestyle-related diseases, and the value of yoga as a health-promoting activity. Involvement of family physicians in health education has been done by a private WONCA Foundation. Greater systematisation of these efforts by all medical colleges would strengthen health education efforts in the country. In India, 136 medical schools admit more than 6,000 postgraduate trainees in their programmes. Involvement of postgraduate physicians in health education would also be quite beneficial. There is a need to organise health education and health educators in India. A professional organisation and a system of credentialing health educators on the pattern similar to United States would go a long way in strengthening the profession and quality of health education.

Delivery of health education programmes as vertical programmes relying on techno-managerial approaches has been pointed by some thinkers particularly Banerjias a potential threat. Banerji points out that delivery of several programmes such as Universal Immunisation Programme (UIP), control of diarrheal diseases, acute respiratory infections, AIDS, tuberculosis, leprosy, malaria have been a dismal failure because these programmes fail to build the essential infrastructure at the grassroots level and merely provide "band-aid" kind of token solutions. In the midst of a "behaviour change campaign" half of all sputum-positive tuberculosis patients in a community had sought help from health institutions, where they were summarily dismissed with bottles of useless cough mixture. There is a definitive need to alleviate poverty and improve basic infrastructure in order for health education to be successful. Health education in the Indian context has been criticised as "motivational manipulation.

Health Educational Strategies

All members of the school community need clean air to breathe, clean water to drink, a safe place for recreation, a safe way to travel to school, and protection from extreme temperatures and ultraviolet radiation. A safe and healthy physical environment requires a good location and safe buildings; protection from excessive noise; natural light; appropriate water and sanitation facilities; clean indoor air; a healthy outdoor environment; and healthy school-related activities including safe management and maintenance practices, use of non-toxic cleaning supplies, careful use of pesticides, vector control, and use of non-toxic art supplies. Though some matters of environmental health must be decided, managed and enforced by authorities at the highest levels of government, an informed and motivated group of school/community members can achieve a great deal, at little or no cost, at the local school level. Education plays a key role in efforts to mobilise participation in effective and sustainable action to protect and improve the physical environment of a particular school.

A majority of children throughout the world now attend primary school, which means they spend a significant amount of time within school environments during critical stages in their development. As expected, the physical environment of a school impacts the health of both its students and staff, with consequences that are not limited to the occurrence of immediate illness and disability, but also extend to the development of diseases with longer latency periods and include effects on related matters such as school enrolment, attendance and learning. Potential risks at school include unsafe water and sanitation, contaminated indoor and outdoor air; unsafe building structures; vector-borne diseases such as malaria, yellow fever and dengue fever; excessive exposure to ultraviolet radiation from the sun; and facilities that are contaminated with asbestos, organic solvents, bacteria and toxic metals such as lead and arsenic.

Much can be done to improve physical structures and conditions at the school, however, physical changes alone will not suffice to create a health-supportive physical environment at schools or in communities. Students, and the adults they will soon become, will need to acquire knowledge, attitudes, values and skills to sustain improvements and address new challenges in the environment. Skills-based health education, along with school health policies, school health services and a health-supportive school environment are considered the basic components of an effective school health programme. Actions taken in these four key areas complement and reinforce each other.

Skills-based health education to promote environmental health should:

— increase awareness of environmental threats to health,

— generate a feeling of responsibility for health and the environment,

— inform students about how to avoid health risks and how to create an environment that is conducive to healthy living,

— be designed to contribute to improvements in the physical school environment including the school site and buildings, indoor and outdoor air quality, and school-related activities affecting the environmental quality of schools,

— improve the health of students.

Collaboration between education and health officials, the school health team, the community advisory committee and other school and community members is necessary to identify the knowledge, attitudes, behaviours, skills and services students need to acquire to protect themselves from illness and hazards associated with the physical environment at school or in their communities, and to help improve environmental conditions that affect health. Educational strategies and materials for environmental health-related issues are available through some governmental and non-governmental agencies and organisations, universities, and teachers' unions. Supplemental materials specific to the local environment can be generated by teachers in collaboration with health officials, the school health team, the community advisory committee and other school and community members who can help identify the physical environmental conditions that affect children's health in the community.

The topical issues and learning activities suggested below could form the basis for a unit dealing with environmental health within the overall health education curriculum. Or, where health is not a separate course of study, they could be adapted to fit within other disciplines at various grade levels.

Health Curriculum

Skills-based health education should occur sequentially from primary through secondary levels. It can be taught as a specific subject, as part of other subjects, or as a combination of both. Ideally, it should be part of a comprehensive school health curriculum and integrated into other relevant subject areas. Integrating environmental health issues within existing curricula on health, natural science, social science and the humanities offers opportunities to consider such matters from multiple perspectives and within multiple contexts. For example, in science lessons, students may learn to use scientific methods to identify and measure environmental threats to their own and others' health; in social studies, they might compare the magnitude of specific environmental health problems or the nature and efficacy of solutions proposed in different parts of the world; and in humanities they might look at the ethical and rights issues related to the question of "Whose environment?" Education about the environment can be incorporated into almost any subject, but it should nevertheless also be a core component of the school health education curriculum and a prominent subject in health promotion programmes for staff.

Methods and Materials

A variety of educational methods, including lectures, debates, discussions, experiments, hands-on activities, audio-visual aids, and role-plays are effective tools for environmental health education. These methods should be designed to increase knowledge, build positive attitudes and values, dispel myths, increase skills and provide support for a healthy lifestyle. Methods should be selected on the basis of lesson objectives. For example, a lecture is an effective way to increase knowledge but is less effective in influencing beliefs than discussions or debates. In educating students about the physical environment, practical information that will enable students to reduce their exposure to unhealthy environments and create safe and supportive environments should be emphasised.

Teacher Training

Teachers need to receive training and information to incorporate effectively issues related to health and the environment in their subject area. Teachers could be provided with information about basic relationships between the environment and health, and with learning materials to make the content interesting to their students. They could also be instructed on how to generate a feeling of responsibility toward the environment. Teachers primarily responsible for health and science education could receive training in implementing a curriculum targeted at health issues related to the physical environment of the school and local community. This training could be continuous and address content and teaching strategies.

All teachers should serve as role models for students by demonstrating responsible classroom management practices. They should be encouraged to keep their classrooms healthy by providing adequate ventilation, cleaning them with non-toxic cleaning products, minimising/eliminating mould growth, disposing waste properly, and recycling classroom materials.

Student's Role

Throughout the world, children are the future caretakers of the environment and will become stewards of their own health and that of others. Their knowledge of the environment and their understanding of the relationship between their own health and the environment shape the attitudes children develop toward the environment. One effective way for students to learn about their environment is for them to become active participants in environmental health education. The child-to-child approach, developed at the Institute of Child Health and Education, University of London is based on the observation that children play a central role in the care of their younger siblings and that traditional knowledge and health practices of villages are passed on from parent to child and from child to child. In the child-to-child model, there are four fundamental ways children can serve as health agents for their communities:

— Older children can help younger ones. Children can be taught how to teach their younger siblings to manage their own health.

— Children can learn from others of the same age by doing small projects together.

— Children can pass on health messages that they have learned to the larger community.

— Children can cooperate to create health actions with their communities.

Initiatives for Quality Health Education

As long ago as 1966 a UNESCO meeting of experts recommended 'Health and Hygiene' as one of the six main categories of objectives for primary education in 'developing countries'. This message was reinforced by the concept of Lifelong Education urged by the 1972 report 'Learning to Be', and given greater emphasis at the 1978 Alma Ata conference. Significant milestones have been:

— UNICEF's support for the Child-to-Child movement since its inception in 1999, culminating in the award of the Maurice Pate Prize to Child-to-Child in 1991. UNICEF thus emphasises its commitment to children as partners in promoting health as does UNESCO and the World Health Organisation.

— The increased profile accorded by international bodies led by UNESCO and WHO to school health promotion and education at the 1990 World Conference on Education for All at Jomtien.

— The increased commitment, particularly from WHO during the following decade, to the concept of health-promoting schools with appeals that 'all schools should become health-promoting' and a significant shift of emphasis in the mid-1990s towards emphasis on the health-promoting schools concept at basic education level and in resource-poor countries.

— The growing interest and commitment of all major agencies in the buildup towards the World Education Forum towards placing the issue of school health, including skills-based health education, high on the agenda for discussion and action, a concern which resulted in the launching of the FRESH initiative.

In India, Uganda and Zambia, three important initiatives resulted from such increased commitments. Each deserves special mention because each illustrates an important step forward towards an effective health programme. None realised their full potential and none have survived in their original form, but their significant and positive influences on health education are still extant.

Children for Health Programme, Zambia

Whereas in most other countries the ideas and materials generated by the Child-to-Child movement may have been seen as one of many approaches to health education, in Zambia they initiated a new national policy. Two small local programmes had been operating successfully since 1984, one originated by the Health Sector in Lusaka District and one by the Institute for Christian Leadership, a Catholic education centre in the Northern Province stitute for Christian Leadership. Those working in these two programmes gained access and support for the movement from the President, who launched Child-to-Child Zambia in 1986 as a national movement in which children would become 'freedom fighters for health'.

UNICEF rapidly adopted Child-to-Child as its major health education strategy, mostly based on action from school rather than in school. With the Canadian International Development Agency (CIDA), which was also prepared to invest significantly in health education for teachers, UNICEF also took steps towards introducing health education and the Child-to-Child approach into the school curriculum. Sibeso Luswata, a former deputy director of the National Curriculum Centre, was appointed UNICEF programme officer. Three important inputs ensued. The first was the formulation in 1990 of a Draft Health Education Curriculum for Zambian Training Colleges produced as an outcome of a course for training college tutors. The second was a seminar organised with the Curriculum Development Centre in 1991 in which those involved in drafting the new curriculum for primary schools examined health priorities and the Child-to-Child approach, and considered how they might incorporate them in their new curriculum and materials. The third was the distribution of large quantities of Child-to-Child materials, such as the book Children for Health directly from Child-to-Child in London or modified locally. At the same time, a Zambian-based NGO, WASHE (Water, Sanitation and Hygiene Education), linked with WaterAid, distributed a pack containing many relevant Child-to-Child activity sheets to schools. None of the UNICEF and only a few of the WASHE handouts were directly supported by training.

Meanwhile, throughout the country, Child-to-Child was assumed to be a part of the life and work of all primary schools concentrating mainly, but not exclusively, on health issues. There were Child-to-Child coordinators at provincial and district level, health committees in most schools and some attempts to link colleges with groups of model schools that, in turn, were to influence 'satellite' schools. The scheme was ambitious, under-planned and under-funded, yet it generated considerable enthusiasm in many schools, especially in activities outside the classroom.

Interministerial Panel on Health, Uganda

In 1987, UNICEF promoted the establishment and funded the working of an Interministerial Panel on Health, chaired by a health educator from the Ministry of Health and with representatives from the University, the National Curriculum Development Centre, the Uganda National Examinations Board, UNICEF and WHO. Following a series of meetings, this panel succeeded in drafting primary school and teachers' college syllabuses and in 1988 wrote and published textbooks for health education that were distributed free of charge to a number of schools for use in the syllabus for science and health. With a more reasoned implementation the programme could have made a lasting impact on the curriculum. Content was based on UNICEF health priorities and materials linked to learning in- and out-of-class and promoted the Child-to-Child approach as a regular component of units.

Health Education for School, India

Launched by the Deputy Director at the Ministry of Health and Family Welfare responsible for School Health this workshop and its report were of considerable significance since for the first time senior members of the concerned planning bodies from two ministries, the NCERT and the Central Health Education Bureau (CHEB), were brought together to agree on a common framework for the health education of school-age children. In his Foreword the director of NCERT heralds the meeting as 'a first step towards establishing linkages and coordination between agencies', while in his accompanying Preface the Director General of Health Services describes the document as 'lucid yet precise'.The findings foreshadow many of the arguments presented in this study. The report contains a well-thought-out scope sequence of content, together with a set of objectives for each level divided into cognitive, affective and psychomotor domains. It also includes suggestions that each school develop and progressively revise a health code, and that: activities such as demonstrations, drawing/collection of pictures, skits, drama, roleplay, responsibility for checking health practice(s) of others on a particular day, proper use of the environmental facilities in school may be planned.

The involvement of parents and older children in health promotion and action is emphasised and among the 'long range objectives' each child is asked to do what he/she can individually and collectively to promote:

(i) his/her own health

(ii) health of his/her family members, and

(iii) health of others in the community.

PLANNING OF HEALTH EDUCATION

The health education planned and provided for children in primary school in India, Uganda and Zambia in the year 2000 and notes the inevitable gaps between planning and implementation, intentions and realities. As evidence is compiled from study and visits over the three year period 1998 to 2000 examples and conclusions are based on selective data from the three countries. Over the past ten years responsibility for planning school health has moved from the 'Health' to the 'Education' sectors, although the boundaries are imperfectly drawn. While classroom instruction on health issues is undeniably a matter for 'Education', other aspects of comprehensive school health may still be the responsibility of different sectors.

In Uganda, 'Health' monitors cleanliness of the school environment and runs inter-school competitions. In Maharashtra State, 'Water and Sanitation' organises programmes involving schoolchildren in health promotion activities in their villages. In Zambia, 'Agriculture' sets up programmes to promote vegetable production in schools supported by nutrition education. Such diversity of control is inevitable and often works smoothly and efficiently at local level. At the central level, however, links are often not as close as they should be and are sometimes exacerbated by inter-sectoral competition for scarce resources, such as transport provided by aid agencies. Of major concern are residual difficulties in sharing up-to-date health knowledge between health and education personnel. The latter often know less than they should and vague and out-of date information all too frequently finds its way into syllabuses, textbooks and training manuals.

Within the education sector, responsibility for planning content officially rests with curriculum centres in Africa, and National and State Councils of Education Research and Training in India. Effectiveness of their personnel is however hampered in five ways:

— They have inherited a 'vertical' subject-based panel structure with little 'horizontal' co-ordination across subjects.

— There is a dearth of expertise in primary education in general and in health education in particular.

— Emphasis is on planning classroom syllabuses (and textbooks) and on preparing for examinations... in many ways inapplicable to health.

— Curriculum planning may be isolated from other systems such as those which train teachers and monitor quality in schools. This varies between the three countries involved and is at its most acute in India where the NCERT models a university structure.

— Bodies have an advisory but not controlling role in alternative systems and private schools.

All this weakens their ability to meet the great challenges placed upon them and, in particular, results in differences between the official curriculum and school realities. Alternative structures and projects do exist outside the official primary systems, many of which deliver good health education. These are frequently supported by external agencies. They may involve the community more closely than official systems and may well be more flexible and hence more efficient. However, while these are accepted and sometimes praised by central planners, some of whom may be involved in organising and implementing them, there seems to be little machinery and limited will to allow them substantially to influence central plans.

Despite increased rhetoric advocating devolution of control, there is as yet little machinery for effective content planning at local level in Uganda and Zambia and below state level in India. This reflects two factors: a lack of expertise at this level and reluctance of local bodies to take initiative for fear that they be accused of compromising national standards.

National planning documents, particularly in Africa, reveal the overwhelming consensus that health education in school is considered to be of high priority; this is confirmed in discussions with planners in all three countries. Yet it is also apparent that there are real difficulties in effectively fitting it into current programmes within existing structures and policies.

Aims need to be reflected in content, methods and materials. Examination and assessment strategies need to measure aims and content and a management process needs to be in place to ensure that all this happens in practice and not merely on paper. Even more important is to ensure that all these processes flow down from national to local and school levels.

There is evidence of widespread intent to teach an impressive range of knowledge and skills in health education over a number of school subjects. Unfortunately, in the absence of a national statement this needs to be pieced together from a number of separate sources. National aims for primary education are set out in the preamble of the Uganda primary syllabus but appear in separate documents in India and Zambia. All stress health goals, the emphasis being heaviest in Zambia and lightest in India. General objectives are stated for the different subject syllabuses in which health content appears, but are often framed in different ways and with different emphases. In India there is also an influential document analysing minimum levels of learning at primary stage including, within the area of environmental studies, a master concept 'Understands the factors contributing to the preservation of good health', and a further important reference to attitudinal objectives in schools.

The syllabus documents currently in use in the three countries are:

— The 1988 Primary Education Curriculum in Maharashtra, Standards 1-5. There is substantial health content in three subjects: environmental and general science, physical education and health, work experience.

— The separate subject syllabuses issued by the Zambia Curriculum Development Centre in 1996. There is substantial health content in the social studies, home economics and environmental science syllabuses and some supporting content in Zambian languages and mathematics.

— The 1999 Primary School Curriculum in Uganda for 4 subjects (English, integrated science, mathematics and social studies) issued by the National Curriculum Centre in Uganda. Syllabuses for others, including local languages, were issued two years later.

Health content is anchored in the integrated science syllabus where three of its eight themes, human health, human body, community population and family life, are specifically health related, and reinforced in other syllabuses, notably social studies and English language. What is abundantly evident from this analysis is the heavy emphasis accorded to health in programmes of study. Twenty years before it would have been much less.

A far wider range of topics is also covered. Let us examine the coverage in all three countries of a range of health topics divided into eight categories, namely:

1. Personal hygiene
2. Community hygiene and sanitation
3. Safety
4. Growth and development ('my body')
5. Nutrition and food production
6. Disease prevention
7. Safe lifestyles (including HIV/AIDS awareness)
8. Social health (including population education).

The most logical selection is evident in Uganda where there is one defined carrier subject, integrated science. Whilst in the two other systems a number of subjects share health education content, the amount of time allocated for health content is considerable and coverage is wide. However, an analysis of objectives and content reveals cause for concern.

— Wider behavioural aims defined at national level contract at syllabus level to quite restrictive knowledge objectives. The importance of health education as a means of behaviour change thus becomes weaker as it assumes the status of a series of topics within classroom subjects.

— There is considerable duplication and overlap between and within subjects. It could be argued that issues such as personal hygiene and nutrition are overemphasised.

— There are some notable omissions, particularly within the Maharashtra syllabus, where there is little emphasis on disease prevention and none on disease management (rehydration is, for instance, omitted), no mention of safety in lower classes, no mention of nicotine addiction and no mention whatsoever of HIV/AIDS-related content either in the lower or higher primary syllabus plan.

— Sequencing of items is often questionable, reflecting lack of experience in lower primary education among syllabus developers. Often younger children are asked to carry put activities too difficult for them such as, in the Uganda class 1 syllabus, 'identifying immunisable diseases and outlining their bad effects'. In contrast, some activities suggested for later classes are at times unchallenging and dull.

— Emphasis is on the health of the individual ('my health') rather than on that of the individual as part of a community ('our health'). Much of the content in lower primary levels tends to concentrate on preaching good behaviour rather than maintaining close links between theory in class and action at school and home.

— Syllabus plans are classroom orientated and make no reference to what needs to be taught and learned round the school or taken from school to community. This is especially relevant in Zambia and Uganda where there have been effective Child-to-Child programmes.

— In India, most health education content is concentrated within lower status subjects. Neither physical education and health nor work experience are taken very seriously in schools so that what appears to be a large allocation for health education may, in practice, be confined to very limited coverage within the general science periods.

Most planners now acknowledge that skills-based methodologies are necessary for health education, although there is less consensus on the definition and priorities of the 'skills' to be developed. In Uganda and

Zambia well-publicised programmes emphasise psychosocial life skills and in India 'Joyful Learning'.The Uganda programme is supported by 'Life Skills for Young Ugandans', an innovative guide used with considerable success in training courses run by the team having created it.

Many of the methods recommended in training and teachers' resource books, such as the use and drawing of pictures or charts, the conduct of practical experiments within the classroom or exercises based on working from textbooks, may be impractical within the resource-starved and overcrowded schools, particularly in Africa. Other methods involving the use of the environment round the school, the use of children's home experience as a resource and of children in examining themselves and other children are frequently overlooked or under used. One reason for this mismatch between what is recommended and what is possible lies with the experience of the syllabus writers themselves who not only come from 'richer' environments than most of the children for whom they prepare materials but who are also, by experience and training, wedded to classroom-bound methods and approaches and reticent about approaches that relinquish direct control of pupils. Whereas it is precisely in such circumstances where children work together in groups, find out from their environment and interact with their families, that there is most room for manoeuvre in difficult situations.

Consider the following analysis of the one health-related theme over three years in the official Maharashtra State science syllabus. Note that teacher-led activities outnumber those which require activity by children by two to one and that even these activities favour direct action by children rather than interpretation and discussion. Writing stories, describing experiences, making up and performing simple plays and role-playing are all key ways to develop life skills, but none are present in the recommended syllabus.

The same conclusion may be drawn from examination of the textbooks provided for most children in India and, in far more limited numbers, in Uganda and Zambia. Owning the recommended science or social studies textbook is rare except in urban or private schools. Textbooks vary in quality. Some series from Uganda are imaginative and provide for a number of practical and environmental activities, supplemented by some excellent English language texts that link language skills with health issues. Sadly the cost of such books, the fact that they are designed to be used by individual rather than groups of children and the language in which they are written precludes their use by at least 80% of the school population. Elsewhere, and particularly in India, books are more pedestrian, classroom bound and sometimes utterly dull.

It has been argued that textbooks can be unnecessary for teaching health education in the first four years of primary school since emphasis should be on direct experience recorded in exercise books. But, school cultures and traditions, reinforced by not-so-subtle pressure from writers and publishers, counter this view. In any case the quality of teachers' guides is very important. Much good resource material is available and some of it, such as the Child-to-Child and WASHE material in Zambia, has been distributed. Unfortunately, it may often be found not with teachers, but stored in cupboards in heads' offices since the inadequate training of teachers often precludes its use. The cost of training for health education is usually beyond governments' means. Thus, it is all too common for the typical teacher to use pupils' books, with all their limitations, to prepare lessons.

Recognition that examinations dictate content taught in primary schools has led African countries to make a conscious effort to examine health education. An analysis of examination questions in Uganda reveals a wide spread of health topics examined. But health education tests typically promote mastery of knowledge whereas health education seeks primarily to modify skills and attitudes leading towards behaviour change, so better methods of evaluating the impact of health education are being actively sought. The use of continuous assessment is frequently mentioned. However, currently such assessment would most likely be undertaken through classroom tests and the latter are usually of poorer quality than expertly set examinations. Experience in Uganda and Zambia suggests that since these are usually set in English this further restricts the scope of what can be measured. However, all three countries are now considering measuring school rather than individual performance, an alternative that will be examined later in this study.

None of the three countries are hostile to the idea of school planning with a view to promoting better health. Indeed, in the limited number of 'Child-to-Child' schools which continue to exist in Uganda and Zambia, health committees and what in Zambia are called 'spearheading groups' remain active. Some schools attached to health projects in Maharashtra also have an identified health coordinator. However, the concept of school health management is unevenly supported and sometimes imperfectly understood, being equated largely with improvement of the school health environment. Action to link 'healthy school' management with curriculum content is all the more difficult because of the divorce of curriculum centres from school management concerns. All too often the programme of studies in schools is considered to be 'academic' and controlled by the education department, and the programme linking school with community as 'practical' and under the control of the ministries of health or water resources, a situation pertaining in parts of Uganda and in rural Maharashtra.

Zambia and Uganda run special shortened patterns of primary schooling to serve children not enrolled in regular schools, e.g. the SPARK programme in Zambia, or the COPE and ABEK programmes in Uganda, many of which give health a more central emphasis than 'mainstream' programmes. However, this seems to result from the omission of other less essential elements from longer programmes in other subjects, rather than from rethinking scope, sequence and methodology in health.

In the southern state of Tamil Nadu in India a small NGO, Health Education and Promotion International, has come up with a complete new syllabus and teachers' manual for health (conceived as a separate subject and integrated within the physical education and health and work experience components of the curriculum). Designed by the NGO's founder and director, a veteran Australian educator, based on a proposal designed for Australian schools, and after having been extensively and conscientiously modified to suit local conditions, the syllabus has been accepted by the state for use in a proportion of its urban schools and limited resources for training teachers have been allocated. Each theme is developed each year through a series of lessons. Each lesson is developed according to a common plan that identifies content and methodology and specifies ways in which the lesson content can be spread by the children in their homes and linked to community action.

Single-issue programmes operate to a greater or lesser extent in all three countries. Some, whilst based on a single concern, extend to cover a number of related topics, for instance, the Schools Health Action and Training Programme (SeHAT) in Delhi and Mumbai that was triggered off by concerns for dental hygiene and then broadened out into issues of nutrition and sanitation. Water and sanitation programmes, in Zambia, Maharashtra and many other states in India, encompass units on prevention and treatment of malaria and diarrhoea.

HIV/AIDS awareness programmes in Uganda develop a whole range of life skills and also focus on child care and development since they are fundamentally concerned with AIDS orphans. Many, if not all, of these programmes have introduced innovatory teaching techniques and some provide in-school training and supervision. This undoubtedly raises quality at the time, but may involve costs that could prove prohibitive once outside support ceases, as was the case with the SeHAT programme. However, most single-issue programmes are taught in parallel to current health education content, rather than being integrated into it. A nutrition programme may teach its own content supported by its own workbook while schools cover the same ground in a more traditional way as part of the science syllabus. If they claim to offer true partnership, then NGO-assisted projects need to focus on the identification of their specific issues within the wider school health programme. On the other hand, national bodies have to recognise that approaching school health in a different way and in a different sequence may help them reach their goals. There appears to be little theoretical difficulty in reconciling such approaches but very considerable communication problems.

4

Environmental Perspectives of Health Education

The role of education both inside and outside school is to build knowledge in such a way as to allow everyone to exercise full, participatory citzenship. However, democratization of education is an essentially political issue rather than merely a pedagogic one, a fact which is conditioned by the distribution and acquisition of wealth, going beyond the limits of educational activity and those of the school itself. This underscores the obstacles faced by any educational program in Brazil in view of government inertia in relation to urgent social change, without which any initiative will always be of limited reach.

One cannot hardly believe that education alone is capable of promoting changes at the structural level of society. However, education plays the fundamental role of favoring a critical reassessment of content and therefore of opening perspectives for demands in a democratic sense, i.e., in the sense of greater participation in choosing one's own destiny and managing the social context.

History points to an evolution from traditional health education to more recent innovative proposals. The traditional view determines what should be done and learned without considering a population's reality and felt health needs. Thus, the objective of traditional Health Education is to promote hygienie habits, basic child care, the use of cleaning materials and procedures, and adequate nutrition, emphasizing the question of sickness either by fostering preventive attitudes or recognition of initial signs of illness and awareness of treatment options.

Increased social awareness has revealed the inadequacy of this type of education as to the following:

1) links with political interests other than those of the populations themselves;
2) its technical character, incapable of promoting changes in attitude by operating solely on the basis of vertically transmitted scientific knowledge; and
3) historical inertia, fossilized in outdated educational practices and contents.

Effective Health Education requires recognition of popular wisdom and practice in search of solutions to problems, a steady updating through continuous influx of constantly changing technical-scientific information, and emphasis on health promotion and improvement of quality of life. This implies a critical perception and attitude on the part of the educator, a command over relevant information in his/her area and intrinsic motivation for the work he/she carries out.

It is of fundamental importance that educators be involved in participatory education where technical knowledge and popular wisdom complement each other knowledge is not produced exclusively by those who teach but is also based on practice: "knowledge is born and develops as people reflect on the experiences lived in all practices.

Approaching the concept of health and illness in the school thus generates reflection on the various dimensions involved in these concepts, and on their complex and multifaceted nature. According to Novaes, health and illness are much more historically situated social values than a simple expression of the body's biological context in a given environment, and they should thus be interpreted in terms of their historical aspect.

Considering that disease occurs in a given environment, Rouquayrol emphasizes that the final state leading to a disease is the result of synergistic action amongst a multiplicity of political, economic, social, cultural, psychological, genetic, biological, physical and chemical factors. To formulate a concept of disease is not simply a matter of knowing how to define it. It implies an understanding of its history, its consequences, and especially its complex determinants which the educational system often reduces to simple etiological agent-host interactions.

Reforms in school curricula starting in the late 1980s indicate a new view of health, seek articulation with other fields, and contemplate the environmental and socioeconomic aspects related to health. Now, in the early 1990s, with an increased worldwide awareness as to the effects of ecological imbalance on the human species, health is being considered within a broader context, contemplating its relationship to both the physical and social environment. This approach has led to changes in school curricula content and has sparked new attitudes in teachers. Hopefully, this will be not merely a passing trend but an effective, long lasting advance in education.

Education considers the individual a real ecosystem or microcosm. His body is a microbiotic system which or may not live in harmonious association. When a disturbance or imbalance occurs amongst elements of a biological system or between individual and their environment, the result is what we call disease.If man is understood as an ecosystem integrated with the total environment, he will develop positive values, attitudes and relations with this environment only if he also develops these positive values towards himself.Thus, from the onset, it is vitally important to stimulate a positive self-image in children, leading them to value themselves and to perceive that they are part of a larger context.

Children should learn that each action they perform may provoke a reaction in somebody else or in the environment, which in turn will probably produce a response.

Knowing the facts and concepts about the environment helps a child to acquire undestanding and to develop social awareness (positive attitudes) which will affect behavior (necessary actions) toward the environment as whole. It is essential to help pupils to develop responsibility in terms of conservation of their own body, their house, their world. And this process will be successful only if it occurs in an affective climate without external impositions but offered with pleasure and understanding. Thus, the approach to health in the school should involve the affective and cognitive domains. Side by side with concrete and direct experiences, the acquisition of new information and of essential facts can situate classroom studies in a creative perspective, favoring the discovery of certain phenomena by the pupils themselves.

It is necessary to alternate situations of teaching about the problems and their solutions with practical experiences that may permit children to develop the "sense of wonder",which means love for one's existence on a planet so full of wealth and fascinating landscapes.

This positive side of Environmental Education should bě counterbalanced with information about the threats endangering natures, since it is important to learn to deal with these facts.

One of the strategies that could be used in the school is the stimulation of children to become involved in the environmental problems of their own community, searching for collective solutions.This emphasizes the role of the school, in which the educational process has a better guarantee of continuity and consistency, since the educational programs included in campaigns are of a transitory nature and utilize only mass communication media, with a consequent reduction of effectiveness.

Considering the low education level of most of the Brazilian population and the high drop-out rate, children are likely to be found in school only in the first grades of elementary school, when Health Education is of the greatest importance and can play a highly valuable role.

As pointed out earlier, for an educational program to be successful, it is necessary to consider the reality of the students and of their community, their habits, beliefs, cognitive characteristics, interests and motivations. When addressing children and adolescents, it is important to be alert to their developmental phase, to investigate their intuitive concepts of health and sickness, their perception of reality, so as to avoid any dissonance, conflict or inefficacy of information.

For the process to be permanent and not simply of an interventionist nature, it is necessary to invest in teacher training, stimulating the formation of a critical conscience. Thus, the teacher, and not somebody from outside the community will trigger an enriching educational action though a type of work is also political in that" learning about health is to learn to live", as recommended in the book "Saúde comocompreensão de vida" ("Health as an understanding of life") coordinated by Hortência de Hollanda. From this perspective, technical information should be associated with a discussion of the way of life and the rights of citizens, of a participation and organization that will lead to the conquest of rights to public services, to work and well-being, as suggested in the chapter "For an understanding of health":

> "No matter how simple they may appear to be, the perceptions of the pupils are paths that will lead them to the necessary knowledge about health. Starting from these perceptions, they will become aware of the relations existing in their community or region between the ways of life and the level of health, to the discovery and categorization of the factors that condition health or sickness, to an understanding of the world that surrounds them, where not only people but also other living beings such as animals, plants and mocroorganisms, hare with them the space for life, revealing the same basic needs for food and shelter and behaving with remarkable powers for adaptation and for the struggle for survival".

For this perspective to be reached in the schools, it is necessary to offer courses to teachers, since, as observed earlier, their pedagogic efficiency and broad and critical vision of the health question is essential to motivate the participating and creative action of the students.

The experience of Schall et al. has demonstrated that training courses including a combination of theoretical classes and practical activities are more effective. Thus, basic content on health should be combined with texts on teacher-pupil relations, pedagogic methods and the use of artistic and cultural resources. After each unit, the teachers should demonstrate how to teach about health using different creative activities such as games, stories, dramatization, puppet theatre, shows, excursions and handcraft techniques, all of them related to the health questions of the community to which the school belongs.

It is important to stimulate teachers to plan and execute practical projects together with the students. Projects that investigate some health problems which are relevant to the students and to the school region and]including actions and alternatives forsolutions represent the proposal of the Laboratory of Environmental and Health Education. The teachers are stimulated to recor their experience, to accompany it bysystematic evaluations and to present it at scientific-pedagogic events. Thus, both teachers and pupils are stimulated to work creatively, developing and valuing the attitude of scientific observation and analysis of phenomena, determining the effect of their practice through the evaluations and becoming affectively involved with their schoolmates and the environment. In this respect, by intermingling with the other disciplines in the curriculum, environmental and health education brings a new dimension to the school, emphasizing human relations and the interaction of man with the environment from a harmonious and dynamic perspective of a commitment to social justice.

Healthy School Environment

Children living in poor populations in rural and peri-urban areas in developing countries are particularly affected. These children face health risks from living in an environment that lacks clean air, water, and food, and from hazardous chemicals associated with rapid economic and urban development. Children are more susceptible to the harmful effects of chemical, biological and physical threats in their environment for the following reasons:

— Children are in a dynamic state of growth and their nervous, immune, respiratory, endocrine, reproductive and digestive systems are still developing. Their ability to detoxify and excrete toxins differs from that of adults. Exposure to environmental toxicants during certain stages of development can irreversibly damage the normal development of organs and systems.

— Young children breathe faster, and eat and drink more in proportion to their body weight than adults. They drink 2.5 times more water, eat 3 to 4 times more food, and breathe 2 times more air. Children therefore absorb more toxicants contained in air, water or food, which makes them more vulnerable to acute and chronic effects of environmental hazards.

— Children often have a greater exposure to environmental hazards than adults: they are closer to the ground where many contaminants settle and young children commonly put their hands into their mouths.

— The longer lifespan of a child increases the risk of developing diseases with long latency periods such as cancer.

Around 1.1 billion people lack access to improved drinking water sources. Even sources of water thought to be safe may be affected by microbiological or chemical contamination. For example, where the water distribution systems in urban areas function intermittently, contaminated water may infiltrate into the pipelines. In Bangladesh as well as many other parts of the world, contamination of groundwater with arsenic is a major public health problem.

The Global Water Supply and Sanitation Assessment reported that 2.4 billion people globally did not have access to any type of improved sanitation facilities in 2000. These facts indicate that billions of people around the world, especially the poor, are at serious risk of contracting diseases such as diarrhoea, intestinal parasitic infections, trachoma, schistosomiasis, and of being exposed to high concentrations of heavy metals or chemicals.

For many children, much of their school day is spent indoors. The air they breathe inside their school may be more polluted than outdoor air. Poor indoor air quality may increase rates of asthma, allergies, and infectious and respiratory diseases, and affect student performance of mental tasks involving. In many rural schools in developing countries, fuels such as dung, wood and coal are used for heating and the preparation of school meals, exposing students to high levels of particles and other toxic pollutants.

Cooking and heating with simple fuels is likely to be the most prominent source of indoor air pollution in developing country schools but additional pollutants may include airborne bacteria and viruses, molds and fungal growths, and particles from building materials. In schools in industrialised countries, indoor air pollution may be the most prevalent of all environmental hazards. Over half of the schools surveyed in the United States reported at least one environmental problem affecting indoor air quality.

Problems include molds and toxic fungi; pesticides; volatile organic chemicals emitted from cleaning products, photocopiers, and classroom furnishings; radon gas and outdoor pollutants entering the school buildings; airborne asbestos from insulation, and lead released from paints and other building materials. Faulty heating, ventilation, and air conditioning systems can exacerbate air quality problems. "Sick building syndrome," manifested by headaches, nervous system effects, and respiratory problems, is routinely reported to American school nurses. The syndrome became prevalent in the 1970s and continues today with the construction of airtight buildings designed to conserve energy.

In urban settings, children are exposed to outdoor air pollution from industry and traffic exhaust fumes on their way to school, and outdoor air pollutants may enter into the classroom. These health effects are difficult to quantify, but WHO estimates that worldwide about 800 000 annual deaths and 0.8% of all DALYs are caused by outdoor air pollution. Air pollution is a global health threat to children. Nearly 80% of 105 European cities surveyed exceeded WHO air quality standards for at least one pollutant.

In Western Europe, asthma cases have doubled in the last ten years. In the United States, the number of asthmatics has leapt by over 60% since the early 1980's and deaths have doubled to over 5 000 per year. In the Russian Federation, over 200 cities often exceed pollution limits and air pollution has been implicated as a contributing factor to 17% of childhood illnesses. Air pollution in developing world cities is estimated to be responsible for 50 million annual cases of chronic coughing in children younger than 14 years of age. In Beijing, Delhi, Jakarta, and Mexico City, pollution levels sometimes exceed WHO air quality standards by a factor of three or more.

In some of China's major cities, particulate levels are as much as six times the WHO guidelines. Throughout the world, as many as 1.5 billion urban residents breathe air exceeding WHO air quality standards. While all school children incur health risks as a result of exposure to air pollution, children with asthma need to be particularly concerned because they are 40% more likely to have an asthma attack on high outdoor pollution days. Even short-term increases in air pollution levels have been associated with an increase in asthma symptoms in children.

The majority of lifetime sun exposure for most people occurs during childhood. Ultraviolet radiation exposure and sunburn during childhood constitute an important risk factor for several long-term health effects, among them skin cancer and cataracts. Damage is preventable through sensible sun exposure behaviour. It is important to target children's attitudes and behaviour at a young age, particularly during primary school, when they tend to be most receptive. Preventive health habits developed at a young age may persist into adulthood and can enable healthy adulthood and ageing. Schools are vitally important settings to promote sun protection, as during the first 18 years of life a significant proportion of time is spent at school where sun exposure may occur.

Children may be particularly sensitive to the cancer-causing and other adverse effects of pesticides, and accumulate a large percentage of their lifetime health risk during childhood. Exposure to pesticides at school may result from their application both indoors and outdoors. Children in both developing and industrialised countries may also be exposed to pesticide residues in drinking water, food and objects such as books and toys. Pesticides are widely misused due to misunderstanding of their toxicity by applicators. Labels rarely provide a complete and accurate summary of pesticide health threats. Pesticides like DDT have been banned or restricted in many countries, but are still widely available in others. In a school in Costa Rica for the children of workers in a banana plantation, health problems were reported to be overwhelmingly respiratory and eye infections. The school was located in the center of the plantation and was regularly sprayed with insecticide from the plantation's aircraft.

Several recent studies in various parts of the United States found that nearly 85% of schools were treated with pesticides, with no notification or vacancy requirement prior to spraying. Some of the pesticides used have the potential to cause short-term or longterm health effects, including vomiting, diarrhoea, convulsions, headaches, skin irritations, liver damage, neurological problems, and behavioural and emotional disturbances. Other pesticides used in schools were labelled with warnings of health effects that may include reproductive system disorders, flu-like symptoms and asthma-like problems. In addition to using pesticides in and around school grounds, many industrialised countries use "pressure treated lumber" that has been impregnated with pesticides to build play sets and picnic tables. In the United States, new regulations on pressure treated lumber will help avoid this problem in the future.

In 2002, UNESCO estimated that nearly 5 500 children die each day from bacteria in food. Unsafe food remains a widespread public health problem in all parts of the world. Surveys in New Zealand, Europe, and North America suggest that each year up to 10% of the population suffer from diseases caused by unsafe food. *E. coli* bacteria are a major cause of diarrhoea and kidney failure that can be fatal in children. The largest ever outbreak occurred in 1996 in Japan, affecting 6 300 school children and 92 staff members and resulting in two deaths. The probable cause was determined to be fresh radish sprouts. Another large *E. coli* outbreak occurred in Africa: contaminated drinking water and cooked maize infected thousands of people. In developing countries, a polluted environment, lack of a safe water supply and poor sanitation increase the likelihood of food contamination. Worldwide, most outbreaks result from improper food handling such as use of contaminated equipment; contamination by infected persons; use of contaminated raw ingredients; cross-contamination; and addition of toxic chemicals or use of food containing natural toxins.

Lands near or directly beneath schools in many parts of the world may pose health threats to children. Schools located near transportation corridors, bus depots, industrial sites, abandoned lots, landfills, military bases, utility plants, and construction sites may present health problems to the students and staff occupying the school. New schools are difficult and expensive to site and are often constructed on undesirable lands. In developed countries, enormous sums of money are spent remediating schools that have been built on hazardous land. Many schools are located adjacent to highways causing students' and staff's exposure to high concentrations of vehicle exhaust, which is known to contain several cancer-causing substances and at least 50 toxic air pollutants.

There are potentially many changes that can be implemented to improve a school's physical environment and, ultimately, the health of students and staff. These changes can serve to educate students, teachers, and parents about the relationship between the environment and health. For example, providing shade from a sweltering sun either by planting trees or building shade structures and encouraging the use of clothes, hats and sunglasses can reduce exposure to the damaging effects of ultraviolet radiation.

Minimising the use of pesticides in schools while educating teachers and students about why this is important can lead to a heightened awareness about the hazards of pesticides in the community. Implementing changes in the physical environment to improve indoor air quality with the goal of reducing respiratory illness and asthma will educate students about managing their own environment to improve respiratory health. Students can, in turn, educate their parents about these management techniques. Health education activities brought home from school by children have been found to positively influence parents' self-management of asthma.

Schools can implement policies and procedures that can improve the health of students at little or no extra cost. Some examples include:

— Reducing risk of diseases such as malaria, dengue fever and schistosomiasis by improving drainage to eliminate formation of puddles where mosquitoes and other vectors breed.

— Adjusting behaviour to avoid risks. Scheduling outdoor activities during periods of the day when air pollution and sun exposure are lowest and insects are not feeding can reduce children's exposure to toxic air pollution, ultraviolet radiation, and insects that transmit diseases.

— In areas where school children cross busy roads, crossing guards or older children can assist younger children and reduce the risk of accidents.

— Prohibiting the idling of school bus engines can minimise exposure to diesel and gasoline exhaust fumes. Buses should not idle in areas around schools where fumes could enter the school building.

— In the developing world, where children dip unwashed hands into a shared drinking water source, a ladle may be used to fill cups or bowls providing a low-cost solution to cleaner water.

— Teaching young children basic rules of food safety such as washing hands before eating.

— Establishing safety rules in the handling and preparation of foods.

— Planting shade trees around school grounds to reduce the risk of overexposure to the sun's ultraviolet rays.

— Creating a health committee with a mission to ensure that classroom facilities and grounds are safe and healthy for children.

- Sorting and recycling waste.
- Reducing respiratory infections by using improved stoves and increasing ventilation when polluting fuels are used inside schools for cooking and heating.
- Reducing asthma attacks by improving ventilation to enhance indoor air quality. Depending on the location of the school, ventilation in classrooms may often be improved by simply opening a window. Where resources permit, additional options can be considered.
- Reducing pesticide exposure and poisonings by eliminating/minimising use of pesticides. Schools adjacent to locations where pesticides are routinely applied could learn about the timing of pesticide applications and keep children inside the school with windows and doors closed.

In the developing world, providing separate sanitation facilities for girls is an important contributing factor in reducing dropout during and before menses. Educated girls marry later in life, have fewer children and are more likely to seek health care for themselves and their children. An increase in the number of girls who stay in school is likely to lead to a reduction in childhood mortality, improved children's health and nutrition, and a deceleration in population growth. Female education has the greatest return on the dollar of all investments available in the developing world. Eliminating air pollutants that trigger asthma attacks and other respiratory illnesses can help improve attendance in high and low income nations. In the United States, asthma is believed to be the most common reason that students miss school.

Building capacity to protect children's health and educational potential will demand changing knowledge, perspectives, and priorities. It will also require collective decisions to adopt new policies, and make commitments to pursue specific plans for health risk reduction. Procedural steps toward creating a healthy physical environment at schools are:

— *Participation*: Organise broad participation to design and implement plans to create healthy school environments. Participants could include school administrators; managers of facilities, transportation and grounds; parents; students; community leaders; and experts in public health and environmental protection.

— *Threat identification*: Conduct research to identify the magnitude and relative importance of significant threats to health within the school environment. Threats may be associated with the following: water quality, sanitation, air quality, food safety and nutrition, vector-borne diseases, waste management, pesticide use, hazardous chemical management, transportation, adjacent land uses, structural integrity, renovation, purchasing, and grounds management.

— *Goal identification*: Establish clear and measurable goals to reduce significant threats.

— *Design of intervention plans*: Design specific intervention plans to improve healthpromoting practices in the following areas: water quality, sanitation, air quality, food safety and nutrition, waste management, pesticide use, hazardous chemical management, transportation, facility siting, structural integrity, renovation, purchasing, and grounds management.

— *Implementation of plans and evaluation of progress*: Implement the intervention plans. Define timetables to meet goals, and assign clear responsibility and accountability. Routinely evaluate progress in goal attainment, and the effectiveness of interventions. Adjust policies, intervention plans, and methods of implementation in response to evaluations, changing conditions and availability of resources.

PROTECTIION OF SCHOOL ENVIRONMENT

Successful protection of children from environmental threats at school requires careful definition of problems and goals to resolve them. Goals are grouped into two categories: substantive goals and procedural goals.

1. Substantive goals
   - *Hazard reduction:* Reduce exposure to significant physical, biological and chemical threats to children's health within the school environment.
   - *Education*: Educate school administrators, teachers, parents, health providers, political leaders and community members about direct and indirect relationships between the school environment and health.
   - *Surveillance:* Create an effective system to monitor and record infectious and chronic disease prevalence, and environmental hazards within the school environment.
   - *Health service delivery:* Develop capacity to provide fundamental emergency medical care within each school.
   - *Food:* Provide safe and nutritious meals for students.
   - *Water:* Provide safe water at schools for drinking, cooking and washing.
   - *Sanitation*: Provide clean and well maintained sanitary facilities, separate for males and females.

— *Transport:* Provide safe passage between homes and schools.

— *Waste:* Create a secure and effective system for waste collection, storage and removal.

— *Facilities:* Ensure structural integrity of school buildings, use of safe building materials, and health protective renovation procedures.

— *Grounds*: Prevent students from exposure to dangerous conditions on grounds, such as rivers, ravines, flood prone areas, rockslides, or highways. Manage grounds to prevent diseases carried by rodents or insects.

— *Hazardous materials storage:* Ensure that hazardous materials are stored safely and securely, preferably in a structure detached from educational facilities. Hazardous materials include fuels, solvents, some cleaning supplies, paints and wood finishes, pesticides, and vehicle fluids.

— *Pesticides:* Restrict use to situations where pesticides will confer a health protective benefit, such as reducing insects that carry diseases, and then employ only the least toxic alternatives.

— *Tobacco:* Eliminate use of tobacco on school grounds.

— *Green purchasing:* Develop criteria to guide purchasing of products and services that will better protect the environment and children's health. Categories of products for which low risk options should be identified include: food, vehicles, fuels, furnishings, cleaning products, building materials, pesticides, paints and wood finishes.

2. Procedural goals
   - *Participation:* Create decision-making processes that encourage broad community participation in goal formulation, policy development, intervention design, implementation and evaluation.
   - *Transparency in decision-making:* Make decisions and deliberations in open meetings.
   - *Freedom of information*: Information and records on hazards in the school environment should be publicly accessible.
   - *Protection of privacy*: The privacy of individual medical records should be protected.
   - *Fair warning of significant hazards:* If school officials recognise unusually hazardous situations, the community should be promptly warned.
   - *Timely response*: The community should expect a timely response by school officials to credible evidence of health hazards.
   - *Equity:* Implement interventions to achieve an equitable reduction in exposure to hazards within school environments.

Health-promoting Policies and Activities

A school health team may be designated to coordinate and monitor health-promoting policies and activities. If a school does not have a health team, planning to improve the school's physical environment can provide the opportunity to form one. Valuable members of the school health team could include teachers, administrators, school nurses, students, parents, transport managers, facilities managers and groundskeepers. Specific task forces can be organised to focus on specific health concerns such as health surveillance and evaluation, health service delivery, sanitary facilities, water quality, food preparation and safety, waste management, transport, vector-borne disease management, pesticide use, structural facilities, renovation, purchasing, and grounds.

Planning improvements to the physical environment provides an opportunity to work outside the school with those who have an interest and expertise in the relationship between the environment and health. Potential partners from the community include parents, childcare centers, local government representatives, businesses, residents, non-governmental agencies, health service providers, environmental organisations, and experts in facility design, construction, renovation, grounds management, waste management, transport, and infectious diseases. The community advisory committee could:

- Identify specific problems and goals;
- Provide expertise for design and implementation of intervention plans;
- Disseminate information about environmental health issues, in particular regarding children;
- Encourage broad community involvement and support;
- Search for financial support and voluntary contributions to meet the goals of the intervention plans.

Schools could develop intervention plans that include:

- *Purpose statement:* A general purpose statement should address the need for hazard reduction, environmental quality, safety assurance, education, surveillance, and health service delivery.

— *Problem identification*: Problems should be identified and ranked in order of relative significance to provide priorities given limited budgets and time.

— *Goals and objectives*: General goals and specific objectives should provide clear and measurable targets for environmental improvements.

— *Procedural policies:* Policies should be adopted to structure participation, transparency in decision-making, access to information, confidentiality and privacy of medical records, warning of significant hazards, timely response to significant threats, and equitable reduction in exposure to hazards within school environments.

— *Specific intervention strategies:* Specific strategies should be designed to protect or improve the following components of the school environment: nutrition and food safety; water quality; air quality; sanitation facilities; transportation; waste; facilities design, construction, renovation and maintenance; grounds; hazardous materials storage; pesticide use; and purchasing.

— *Educational strategy:* Each plan may also include an educational strategy, addressing important problems through curricular and extracurricular efforts.

— *Responsible parties*: Specific individuals should be assigned responsibility to develop and implement components of intervention plans.

— *Financial analysis*: Each plan should include a financial analysis estimating the cost of goal attainment, and potential sources of funding or voluntary service and materials.

— *Evaluation*: Each plan should include criteria for evaluating progress and goal attainment.

— *Community outreach*: Each plan should consider how the expertise, labour and financial resources of community members might be helpful in achieving goals.

Both qualitative and quantitative data are necessary for planning effective environmental health interventions, and to establish a baseline for evaluation. Qualitative data include perceptions, beliefs, and attitudes; quantitative data include numerical information.

COMMITMENTS

Making improvements to a school's physical environment will require understanding and commitment from a wide range of individuals and groups, including relevant government departments, health and education authorities, community and business leaders, educators, parents, students, and the community. Successful reduction of environmental health threats within schools demands political commitment at all levels of government. Political leaders will need to understand the importance of the threat. Experience in some nations suggests that recognition of school environmental health problems results from the educational efforts of community and grass roots organisations. National legal authority, expertise, and financial support may be necessary to implement change, especially within the poorest communities. Political commitment and support may occur in the form of:

— *Support for research*: Research to understand more fully the extent and distribution of environmental health threats faced by children in schools is often necessary. Although hazards may vary from classroom to classroom, national and regional governments and universities can show commitment by providing support and/or expertise to implement needed research. Results of such research can also be publicly acknowledged and disseminated by national authorities.

— *Authority and responsibility*: National authority to set standards for physical school improvements may be necessary to bring about significant change. This authority could require the provision of safe food and water; attainment of sanitary standards; and establishment of pollution limits and building standards.

— *Financial commitment*: Financial support for construction, maintenance, health surveillance, medical services, and environmental hazard assessment and intervention may all be necessary to assure sufficient health protection for children in schools. Training, equipment, and materials may be required to enable schools to develop and implement physical improvements. Many communities lack the financial resources necessary to provide these services, and will need financial commitments from provincial or national levels.

A healthy school environment requires community support. Parents and community members need to participate in the development and evaluation of interventions to improve school health. Commitment and the support of many parties on a variety of levels are necessary to share expertise, facilities, and resources. Community group meetings, parent-teacher conferences, open houses, and formal presentations are all opportunities for involving family and community members early in the development process. Community commitment may be enhanced by:

— Public recognition of the association between health and the environment by community leaders, local government representatives, health and education authorities, and other relevant organisations.

- — Establishment of a designated committee for coordinating efforts to improve the physical environment of schools.
- — Provision of local resources for interventions to improve the physical environment of schools.
- — Coordination of interventions with other programmes in the community.
- — Efforts to attract community and media attention.

Integrated Health Education

A health-promoting school draws on the school's full organisational capacity to improve the health of students, school personnel, families and community members by improving the physical environment of the school and educating the school community about environmental health threats. Physical improvements to schools can serve as an entry point for the development or enhancement of policies, planning groups, and various components that serve as a framework for a health-promoting school.

The effectiveness of interventions integrated into each of these components is influenced by the extent to which they are supported by a variety of people, policies, and trained staff and by the extent to which interventions in each of these components combine with other health promotion efforts to complement and reinforce each other. Most schools will not have the resources to address all the environmental health issues that might be identified at once. Each school must establish its own priorities, in collaboration with all parties concerned, to decide the extent to which identified issues should be addressed.

A health-promoting school should enable students, parents, teachers and community members to work together to make these decisions. Schools should start with small changes that are feasible rather than waiting until resources become available to address all of the issues at once.

Skills-Based Education

Physical changes alone will not suffice to create a health-supportive physical environment at schools or in communities. Students, and the adults they will soon become, will need to acquire knowledge, attitudes, values and skills to sustain improvements and address new challenges in the environment. Skills-based health education, along with school health policies, school health services and a health-supportive school environment are considered the basic components of an effective school health programme. They are complementary and reinforcing of each other.

Skills-based health education should increase awareness of environmental threats to health, generate a feeling of responsibility for health and the environment, and improve the health of students. It should inform students about how to avoid health risks and how to create an environment that is conducive to healthy living. It should be designed to contribute to improvements in the physical school environment including the school site and buildings, indoor and outdoor air quality, and school-related activities affecting the environmental quality of schools.

Collaboration between education and health officials, the school health team, the community advisory committee and other school and community members is necessary to identify knowledge, attitudes, behaviours, skills and services students need to acquire to protect themselves from illness and hazards associated with the physical environment at school or in their communities, and to help improve environmental conditions that affect health.

Skills-based health education should occur sequentially from primary through secondary levels. It can be taught as a specific subject, as part of other subjects, or as a combination of both. It should be part of the school health curriculum, and also integrated into a range of subject areas, as relevant. Integrating ideas on environmental health within existing curricula on health, natural science, social science and the humanities offers opportunities to consider environmental health problems from multiple perspectives and within multiple contexts. For example, in science lessons, students can learn to use scientific methods to identify environmental threats to their health and their family's health, and to find effective ways to reduce such threats.

Even though education about the environment can be incorporated into many subject areas, it should be a core component of school health education classes and a prominent subject in health promotion programmes for staff. Educational materials and teaching strategies for environmental health-related issues are available through some governmental and non-governmental agencies and organisations, universities, or teachers' unions. Supplemental materials specific to the local environment can also be generated by teachers in collaboration with health officials, the school health team, the community advisory committee and other school and community members who can help identify the physical environmental conditions that affect children's health in the community.

A variety of educational methods, including lectures, debates, discussions, experiments, hands-on activities, audio-visual aids, and role-plays are effective tools for environmental health education. These methods should be designed to increase knowledge, build positive attitudes and values, dispel myths, increase skills and provide support for a healthy lifestyle. Methods should be selected on the basis of lesson objectives. For example, a lecture is an effective way to increase knowledge but is less effective in influencing beliefs than discussions or debates. In educating students about the physical environment, practical information that will enable students to reduce their exposure to unhealthy environments and create safe and supportive environments should be emphasized.

Role of Teachers

Teachers need to receive training and information to incorporate effectively issues related to health and the environment in their subject area. Teachers could be provided with information about basic relationships between the environment and health, and with learning materials to make the content interesting to their students. They could also be instructed on how to generate a feeling of responsibility toward the environment.

Teachers primarily responsible for health and science education could receive training in implementing a curriculum targeted at health issues related to the physical environment of the school and local community. This training could be continuous and address content and teaching strategies. All teachers should serve as role models for students by demonstrating responsible classroom management practices. They should be encouraged to keep their classrooms healthy by providing adequate ventilation, cleaning them with non-toxic cleaning products, minimising/eliminating mold growth, disposing waste properly, and recycling classroom materials.

Role of Students

Throughout the world, children are the future caretakers

of the environment and will become stewards of their own health and that of others. Their knowledge of the environment and their understanding of the relationship between their own health and the environment shape the attitudes children develop toward the environment. One effective way for students to learn about their environment is for them to become active participants in environmental health education.

The child-to-child approach, developed at the Institute of Child Health and Education, University of London is based on the observation that children play a central role in the care of their younger siblings and that traditional knowledge and health practices of villages are passed on from parent to child and from child to child. In the child-to-child model, there are four fundamental ways children can serve as health agents for their communities:

— Older children can help younger ones. Children can be taught how to teach their younger siblings to manage their own health.

— Children can learn from others of the same age by doing small projects together.

— Children can pass on health messages that they have learned to the larger community.

— Children cooperate to create health actions with their communities.

The child-to-child approach is an effective approach to teaching because:

— It links what children learn with what they do;

— It links what children do in class with what they do in the home;

— The activities are not taught in one lesson and then forgotten; they are learned and developed over a long period of time.

The training materials developed by the Child-to-Child

Trust deal with environmental issues such as community-wide water and sanitation surveys, action programmes, and solid waste management schemes.

Creating a Safe School Environment

All members of the school community need clean air to breathe, clean water to drink, a safe place for recreation, a safe way to travel to school to avoid accidents, and protection from extreme temperatures and ultraviolet radiation. A safe and healthy physical environment requires a good location and safe buildings; protection from excessive noise; natural light; clean indoor air and water; a healthy outdoor environment; and healthy school-related activities including safe management and maintenance practices, use of non-toxic cleaning supplies, careful use of pesticides, vector control, and use of non-toxic art supplies.

Before a school is constructed, planners and community groups need to consider potential environmental risks in relation to the school's location, e.g. the vicinity of a chemical plant or former waste site, an area prone to flooding, or a busy, noisy road. Options for improving existing schools on poor sites include hazardous waste removal, construction of footpaths or bridges for getting to school, and construction of school barriers to provide a buffer to hazardous areas. Adjustments in behaviour can be made to account for poor environmental conditions such as avoiding recreation activities during periods of the day when air pollution is at a peak or the sun is most intense.

In areas where school children are required to cross busy roads, crossing guards or older children can assist younger children. If children are required to travel to school by bus, these buses should be in good running order and exposure to diesel or gasoline exhaust fumes should be minimised.

The structure of a school building should protect students and staff, but poorly designed school buildings and play areas may present serious health risks instead. School buildings are often larger than traditional domestic or residential buildings. Special construction techniques may be required to ensure safety, particularly in areas prone to natural disasters such as earthquakes and typhoons. In addition to being structurally sound, school buildings and play areas should be constructed without asbestos and with the safest, non-toxic materials available. Schools should be designed to prevent temperature extremes inside classrooms.

Cold, damp, and poorly ventilated classrooms provide an unhealthy environment for school children, particularly poorly nourished and inadequately clothed students who are especially vulnerable to respiratory and other infections. Extremely warm conditions may reduce concentration and attention span, and can lead to heat-related illnesses including thermal stress, fatigue, and heat stoke. One way to ensure protection from the elements is to plan school holidays so that they coincide with the rainiest, coldest or hottest season. School siting and landscaping can affect interior conditions such as temperature, humidity, lighting, and ventilation. For example,

— Schools in heavily forested settings are often darker, cooler, and damper than those in open areas.

— Schools in depressions, wetland, or adjacent to rivers or other water bodies are normally damp.

Poorly maintained structures may also pose a health threat to children. Cracks in walls, floors, or foundations provide homes for insects such as hookworms, mites and jigger fleas. Broken windows, dilapidated steps, exposed nails, and missing stair rails present obvious hazards and increase the risk of injury.

Water Quality and Sanitation

Fecal material contaminates drinking water. Children dipping their unwashed hands into a shared drinking-water supply provide a typical route of contamination. In areas where this occurs, providing schools with a ladle to dip into water sources may be a low-cost solution to cleaner water. A safe water supply is free from bacteria, parasites, and toxic chemicals. Where there is uncertainty about the quality of the drinking water, it should be tested regularly. If the water has not been chlorinated, it is important to disinfect it through chlorination, boiling or any other acceptable method. Safe storage of water at school and at home should also be promoted.

Where helminth infections are a problem, store drinking water for over 24 hours and then decant to help remove helminth eggs that may have fallen to the bottom of the container. Boiling is an effective way to kill worms, eggs, and other germs that may have contaminated the water. A filtration system made from stones and sand or gauze/filters in guinea worm areas can also be used to make water safe from worms.

In the industrialised world, water supplies at school can be contaminated by chemicals present on-site as a result of former land-use practices, adjacent land uses, or plumbing fixtures. Many school water fountains have lead-soldered or lead-lined tanks. Patterns of intermittent water use from these fountains result in water standing in tanks longer than in typical residential situations, increasing the amount of lead that is absorbed into the water from the tanks. Schools need to be aware of these potential risks and have their water tested regularly.

Human excreta are the biggest source of disease-producing organisms including parasites, bacteria, and viruses. Success in eliminating fecal material from the school environment is dependent on: informed and responsible students; supervision of young students; a fence or structure to stop animals from defecating in areas where children play; toilets conveniently located, reliable, clean, odor-free, private, and well-maintained. Separate facilities for girls can reduce dropout rates during or before menses. A variety of latrine systems are used in different parts of the world depending on cultural, environmental, and economic conditions. Education and health officials need to make sure that construction of latrines is technically appropriate and acceptable.

Air Quality

The quality of indoor air is a function of building ventilation, construction materials used, and pollutants released inside the building. It is also a function of policy, as in the case of environmental tobacco smoke. WHO strongly recommends that schools and their grounds should be completely tobacco free. Breathing environmental tobacco smoke causes serious health problems. It can aggravate allergies and increase the severity of symptoms in children and adolescents with asthma and heart disease. It is also associated with lung cancer because environmental tobacco smoke contains essentially the same cancer-causing substances and toxic agents that are inhaled by the smoker.

In developing countries, the indoor burning of dung, wood and coal for cooking and heating within schools can cause high levels of fine particles in indoor air that can lead to respiratory illness and trigger asthma attacks. Adequate ventilation should be provided whenever possible and students should be educated about the health effects of poor ventilation, and particles and other combustion by-products in smoke. Schools in the developing world can promote the use of improved stoves, ensure that fuel wood is dry, time cooking activities when students are outside, and ensure that smoke is vented away from places where students may study or play.

A study on the causes of indoor air quality problems in schools throughout the developed worldfound that most problems in school facilities could be avoided by:

— Providing adequate outdoor air ventilation on a continuous basis.

— Controlling the space relative humidity between 30% and 60%.

— Providing effective filters to remove fine particles from the outdoor air.

The probability that children with asthma will have an attack is estimated to be 40% higher on high outdoor pollution days, and research indicates that children that play active sports are more likely to develop the disease in polluted cities. Many schools should be concerned with outdoor air quality. Equipped with some knowledge about air quality in their area, schools may choose to avoid involving students in intensive outdoor exercise during periods of high air pollution. Ozone levels usually peak between midday and evening. Avoiding outdoor activities during high pollution periods and in areas adjacent to highways or near other sources of air pollution will help to minimise asthma attacks in sensitive children and other short- and long-term health effects associated with exposure to air pollutants.

Safety of the Play areas

Play areas should be designed to be more than "play" areas. There is an urgent need for children to be able to take part in regular and appropriate physical activity. Schools offer a unique setting to promote and provide opportunities for physical activity as recreation and sport.

Regular and appropriate physical activity is an essential stimulus for children to reach their potential of growth and development. It is necessary for optimal health and functional capacity. It also counteracts disabilities and diseases common to ageing. Regular physical activity helps children and adolescents develop strong muscles and bones, normal body weight, efficient function of the heart and lungs, and skills of movement. To provide an environment that encourages and enables children to engage in regular and appropriate physical activity, schools should:

- provide play areas that are safe and have facilities for physical activity;
- establish and enforce policies and standards for the use of equipment and grounds to prevent physical activity-related injuries;
- provide time during the day for children to have access to play areas for unstructured physical activity;
- provide access to community recreation areas when insufficient space prevents children from regular physical activity on the schools grounds.

Children need to be protected from injuries that could occur outside the school buildings, and areas where children play or exercise should be free from hazards. Busy roadways, water bodies, waste sites, rockslides, and ravines should be considered threats to children. Play areas should not be located near these areas. When selecting wood for playgrounds or outdoor furniture that children and staff will use, avoid lumber treated with chromated copper arsenic, creosote and pentachlorophenol. Potentially toxic levels of arsenic can leach from the wood to the hands of children and contaminate the soil below where children play. Existing treated play sets can be sealed with polyurethane or painted to reduce exposure to toxic wood preservatives.

Planting shade trees around school grounds can reduce the risk of overexposure to ultraviolet radiation for students and staff, particularly when the sun is at its peak. In countries such as Bangladesh, an open-air classroom with a roof may be sufficient to protect students from the sun while enhancing light and ventilation. However, reflection of ultraviolet radiation from light surfaces may still lead to significant exposure.

School Waste Management

Waste generated in schools should be properly disposed to avoid spread of communicable diseases, discourage the presence of pests and other vectors, and prevent human contact with potentially hazardous material. Appropriate practices of recycling and waste disposal in the community should be identified, and students and other members of the school community should follow these practices. Schools should promote methods to eliminate, conserve or recycle hazardous materials to decrease the volume of hazardous waste generated.

A hazardous waste management plan should be developed to promote the identification, collection and proper disposal of all hazardous waste generated by the school. Many schools in developed countries use mercury containing products such as thermometers, fluorescent lamps and some batteries, possibly placing students and faculty at risk from toxic effects of mercury (mercury is toxic to the central nervous system, digestive system, kidney, liver and skin). Some communities hold annual Household Hazardous Waste Collection Days and school personnel may bring hazardous materials such as batteries and pesticides to these collection events.

Students should be involved in the management of non-hazardous waste at their school to create a sense of responsibility. Students can be involved in collecting waste in the classroom and throughout the school. They can also help to separate waste that can be composted, re-used or recycled. If a system is clearly established to manage waste, the entire school community will be a cleaner and safer environment.

Clean schools have healthier indoor air, a lower risk of spreading contagious diseases, and provide a more pleasant learning environment for both students and teachers. Adequate cleaning requires that areas of responsibility are clearly defined and understood by all members of the school community. Students should be involved in keeping their school clean to create a sense of responsibility and pride in their school environment. Skills, learned in school may be carried into other environments, hopefully for many years.

Schools are easier to keep clean if properly designed. In designing a school, or in upgrading one, clean and dry pathways should lead to the entrance of the school building. If walkways are muddy, students and other visitors to the school will track in mud, dust and outdoor contaminants, increasing the amount of dust in the school and contributing to unhealthy indoor air. Only products that are safe for use around children should be used to clean classrooms. Natural cleansers commonly perform as effectively as harsh detergents and solvents. Use alternatives to products labelled 'caution', 'warning' or 'danger' and use the minimum amount of the product recommended to complete the job.

Managing the use of chemicals within a school is an important issue in industrialised countries. An inventory of chemicals used and stored at school should be maintained, and teachers and staff should understand the risk associated with improperly handling and disposing these chemicals. Chemicals should be stored in a centrally located, secured and ventilated area. In science labs, teachers should eliminate the most toxic chemicals and implement microscale experiments to reduce the volume of materials used or generated.

Indoor use of pesticides leaves residues that may persist long after schools are sprayed. Many nuisance problems can be controlled physically rather than chemically. Screening doors and windows and minimising food crumbs, spills and scraps that attract insects will discourage insects from entering buildings. Schools adjacent to farmland, golf courses, recreational areas or other land uses where pesticides are routinely applied should learn about the timing of application and keep children inside the school with windows and doors closed during periods of spraying. Schools could also encourage nearby pesticide applicators to use alternatives to pesticides. In areas where insect-borne diseases are a problem, schools should employ integrated pest management methods, including the control of water bodies, and develop a pesticide reduction strategy. If these measures are insufficient, the lowest-risk pesticide should be used and guidelines regarding re-entry intervals must be followed.

Health Services

School health services help to treat health problems and to prevent, reduce and monitor them. In a health-promoting school, health services work in partnership with and are provided for students, school personnel, families and community members. School health services should be coördinated with members of the school and community to recognise and treat health problems resulting from exposure to environmental threats. These threats vary from community to community.

School nurses can help raise awareness of health problems among students, teachers and staff, and play an important role in referring students to specialists. They are responsible for "de-worming" at regular intervals, managing health outcomes such as an asthma attack or injury, and recognising severe diseases such as malaria, severe diarrhoea and respiratory infections for correct referral. Ideally, they should receive training in environmental health issues prevalent in their community. School nurses should be responsible for tracking illnesses among students to help identify potential environmental health problems within the school.

A health-promoting school should involve students, school staff, families, and community members in efforts to improve health in the school. Children who participate in efforts to create a cleaner and safer environment learn about protecting themselves and their environment, and can acquire the knowledge, attitudes, values and skills needed to adopt healthy lifestyles as adults. Family and community members can serve on the school health team or community advisory committee; participate in activities and services offered through the school such as helping to build a safe play structure for children or helping to clean up school grounds; or provide support and resources by offering financial or technical assistance to improve a school's building structure or ventilation system. It is important for parents to understand the relationship between their child's health and their environment both at school and at home. A health-promoting school can help to educate parents about potential environmental health threats in the home. This can be accomplished at a school health fair or at a health-related workshop for parents on environmental health threats to children.

5

Comprehensive Physical Education Programme

A comprehensive physical education system helps children and youths achieve three goals. Within each goal appropriate disciplines are addressed to support the knowledge, skills, and attitudes desired for every student. The three goals are equally important; eachinteracts continually with the others in a well-planned programme.

Goal 1: Movement skills and movement knowledge

Disciplines:

— Motor learning

— Biomechanics

— Exercise physiology and physical fitness

Goal 2: Self-image and personal development

Disciplines:

— Human growth and development

— Psychology

— Aesthetics

Goal 3: Social development

Disciplines:

— Sociology

— Historical perspectives.

Skill and Content Areas

The following skill and content areas support the goals of physical education and are introduced at appropriate ages and grade levels. In addition to developing skills in these various areas, students should be encouraged to acquire understanding and knowledge about the content and skills. They should be able to grasp the why as well as the how and to understand that the content areas are a vehicle for developing and refining the skills.

- *Skill areas*
  - *Sensorimotor and perceptual motor.* Examples: kinesthetic, visual, tactile, auditory
  - *Locomotor.* Examples: walking, running, jumping, hopping, galloping, skipping
  - *Nonlocomotor.* Examples: swinging/swaying, bending/stretching, pushing/pulling, twisting/turning
  - *Balance.* Examples: static: stunts, balance equipment; dynamic: tricycle, unicycle, scooter, beams
  - *Eye-hand coordination.* Examples: gross motor: throwing, catching, bouncing; fine motor: pouring, clapping, cutting, grasping Eye-foot coordination. Examples: kicking, trapping, dribbling, punting, rhythmic movement
  - *General coordination.* Examples: swinging, climbing, sliding, jumping rope, tumbling
  - *Creative movement.* Examples: rhythmic walking, swaying, moving to music, mirroring movement
- *Content areas*
  - Rhythms and dance
  - Individual and dual sports

— Aquatics
— Team sports
— Combatives
— Outdoor education
— Gymnastics and tumbling

These skill and content areas are the basis of physical education. For example, developing a sense of rhythm helps children do better in a variety of activities and enhances a sense of flow and coordination. At all levels of the physical education curriculum, the skill areas are taught and reinforced through the content.

Cognitive learning is an inherent part of the skill and content areas. For example, students learn the application of Newton's laws in developing rotational skills, balance, and spin. This knowledge helps to reinforce and strengthen their understanding of the skills and their ability to use them. Throughout the physical education curriculum, children should be encouraged to observe their own and others' behaviour and to process information. Although children do learn through trial and error, they also benefit from guided discovery and development of an understanding of skills and content.

Components

A well-planned physical education programme is one component of a comprehensive school health system. That system, which comprises an organised set of policies, procedures, and activities designed to protect and promote the health and well-being of students and staff, includes the following components:

— Health education physical education
— Health services
— Nutrition services

- — Psychological and counselling services
- — Safe and healthy school environment
- — Health promotion for staff
- — Parent and community involvement

As two components in a comprehensive school health system, physical education and health education should complement each other. However, the ways in which they are separate and distinct must be recognised. Health literacy is "the capacity of an individual to obtain, interpret, and understand basic health information and services and the competence to use such information and services in ways which are health-enhancing." The four unifying ideas are the following:

- — acceptance of personal responsibility for lifelong health
- — respect for and promotion of the health of others
- — an understanding of the process of growth and development
- — informed use of health-related information, products, and services

Physical education focuses on three goals:

- — movement skills and movement knowledge;
- — self-image and personal development; and
- — social development.

Where physical education differs most distinctly from health education is in the emphasis that physical education places on teaching students how to move.

The development of a physically educated person can be compared with the growth of a tree. The roots of the tree correspond to the preschool and primary levels. At this point children are learning the fundamentals of physical education, becoming more skilful, and deriving pleasure from learning new skills through experience with the various content areas. Three fundamentals of physical education that correspond to learning letters in reading and learning numbers in mathematics are central to these levels:

— Locomotion-moving the body from one place to another

— Nonlocomotion-remaining in place and maintaining balance while moving parts of the body

— Object manipulation-including manipulating objects with parts of the body

At the preschool and primary levels, development of physical and motor fitness attributes is emphasized, including agility, flexibility, and coordination. This level emphasizes such basic skills as walking, running, hopping, jumping, sliding, galloping, skipping, catching, throwing, kicking, balancing, bending, and stretching. Also important are such fitness attributes as cardiorespiratory fitness and muscular strength and endurance.

The trunk of the tree corresponds to the upper elementary years. At this level children begin to combine the fundamental skills they have learned in the preschool and primary years and apply and refine the skills in new experiences. At the upper levels of the tree, including the middle school years, children are becoming independent, self-directed learners. They are beginning to internalise the principles of physical education from the earlier grades into a personal commitment to a healthy lifestyle and physical activity. They participate regularly in a variety of physical activities, take pleasure in both group and individual activities, and have begun to formulate a goal of lifelong health. Throughout, the process engages all aspects of learning: cognitive ("I know"); affective ("I feel"); and psychomotor ("I experience and do").

As the tree branches out at the upper levels, high school students are able to choose and participate freely in team sports, individual sports, aquatics, dance, combatives, fitness, tumbling and gymnastics, and other specific aspects of the physical education curriculum. This is an appropriate time for specialising in particular activities, a time when skills learned at the earlier levels become more meaningful and pleasurable in ways that are both satisfying and complex.

Benefits

Physical education offers pupils with learning difficulties opportunities to:

— develop their skills of coordination, control, manipulation and movement,

— enhance appropriate areas of health and fitness and contribute towards their physical development,

— develop their personal qualities of commitment, fairness and enthusiasm,

— develop their thinking, appreciation and evaluation skills,

— compete against themselves and others, and take part in challenging activities,

— develop their ability to express themselves and be creative,

— work individually and as part of a team,

— build their self-confidence and self-esteem.

In response to these opportunities, pupils can make progress in physical education by:

— consolidating, securing, tuning and developing fluency in whatever movements and skills they acquire and develop,

— increasing the range of skills they use in activities,

- improving the control and manipulation of objects,
- improving appropriate areas of health and fitness,
- knowing the different purposes of different types of activity.

Staff should teach knowledge, skills and understanding in ways that match and challenge their pupil's abilities. Staff can modify the physical education programmes of study for pupils with learning difficulties by:

- choosing material from earlier key stages,
- maintaining, practising, consolidating and generalising, as well as introducing new knowledge, skills and understanding,
- using the programmes of study as a resource or to provide a context for planning learning appropriate to the age and needs of pupils,
- focusing on one aspect, or a limited number of aspects, of the age-related programmes of study, such as acquiring and developing technical skills for different purposes.

Skills Development

Acquiring and developing skills begins with pupils becoming aware of themselves and their bodies, tolerating and accepting passive movement, and knowing the different positions and movements they can make. Teaching skills development across key stages can help pupils to:

- explore, develop and establish basic movement patterns and actions they can make, for example, the development of travelling skills that involve moving from one place to another,
- develop coordination and control of their bodies and increase the range of gross and fine skills and movements, for example, whole or part body actions

where movements or actions are performed without travelling, manipulative skills that involve the handling and use of objects and equipment,

— combine and then sequence movements, linking them fluently ,

— move spontaneously and improvise in a range of different activities.

Selecting and applying skills, tactics and compositional ideas begins with pupils exploring the body movements they can make, developing them and applying them to particular purposes.

Teaching this aspect across key stages can help pupils to:

— make choices about what to do and how to do it,

— learn to react to stimuli and move appropriately,

— copy and then repeat actions, for example, using mirrors to watch different parts of their bodies move,

— play, use and understand cause and effect games, for example, predicting their own actions, in,

— games such as skittles, boccia and polybat,

— perform, then combine and sequence actions and change their performance, for example, responding appropriately to different music and tempos, such as relaxing, fast/slow,

— follow and then understand rules,

— use equipment safely for a purpose.

Developing Movement Skills

The most basic element of the student's learning experience in physical education is learning how to move. The physical education curriculum begins, therefore, by addressing the primary goal of achieving movement skills and movement knowledge. A comprehensive physical education programme guides each student in the development of motor skills that allow the student to:

— Move in a variety of ways.
— Learn effective and efficient movement appropriate to the student's changing needs.
— Understand the fundamentals of movement.
— Appreciate the aesthetics of creative movement.
— Enjoy movement for movement's sake.
— Develop all the skills needed to select appropriate activities to develop and maintain a high level of health-related physical fitness.

Movement is the primary medium through which the physical educator reaches and teaches the whole child. Emphasis should be placed on guiding children to discover what they can do. They need to develop proficiency in movement skills so that physical activity will be a successful and enjoyable experience that enhances self-image. Moreover, they should have opportunities to participate in expressive and creative movement leading to greater self-realisation and personal satisfaction. Experiences in physical education can play a powerful role in influencing a student's self-image, which, in turn, influences how that student will feel about continuing participation in physical activity.

Motor Development

Motor learning and motor development together are the basis for how motor skills are learned and what they look like. These concepts can be described in terms of the learner and the learning environment. Motor learning involves development of locomotor skills (e.g., walking, running, hopping, jumping) and nonlocomotor skills (e.g., balancing, bending, twisting, reaching, stretching) and an understanding of the qualities of time, space, force, and flow applicable to those skills. It also involves object manipulation, such as catching, throwing, kicking, and juggling.

Motor learning enables students to master skills in order to perform them consistently and well. It involves feedback, judgment, and trial and error. An example is learning how to take aim and hit a mark. Motor learning is also progressive-for example, learning how to bounce a ball with control before learning to dribble. Motor development refers to what the skills and activities look like in terms of their qualities. Skills and activities can be performed in isolation or as part of a more complex dance, game, sport, or other performance. Motor learning is the how of what students learn, and motor development is the what. In the elementary grades it is particularly important that children receive, interpret, and respond to visual, auditory, tactile, and kinesthetic stimuli for sensorimotor and perceptual motor feedback. Perceptual motor development is a crucial need in the early grades, influencing more than just the child's ability to move. It also has an important influence on readiness for learning.

Biomechanics

Biomechanics is the science that examines the internal and external forces acting on a human body and the effects they produce. It involves the study of how the body moves and how such movement is influenced by gravity, friction, and the laws of motion. Knowing how and why movement occurs and whether it is efficient assists in problem solving and enhances understanding of movement and motor skills. This understanding enables students to modify their performance for skill improvement and determine the most appropriate technique for each motor skill. Key terms include Newton's laws of motion, center of gravity, force projection and absorption, buoyancy, spin, rotational mechanics, levers, vectors, and motion. Through experimentation or guided discovery, students learn that by applying biomechanical principles to physical activity, they can improve their skills and performance.

Exercise physiology

Exercise physiology expands the student's knowledge of the physical self through the study of the human body. Learning progresses from the preschooler's awareness of body parts to the more advanced study of body systems, the ways in which the systems interact, and the effects of exercise on those systems. Students gain an understanding of the importance of developing and maintaining optimum fitness in the areas of cardiorespiratory endurance, flexibility, muscular strength and endurance, and body composition. They learn not only what to do but why to do it and how to do it appropriately and effectively. An important component of exercise physiology is knowing what kind of exercise is needed, how much is needed, and how it is to be performed. Instruction in the principles of physical fitness training should address the issues of frequency, intensity, and time (FIT) as well as specific types of exercise and their effects on the body. It should prepare the student for designing an appropriate personal exercise plan.

Self-Image and Personal Development

Students develop and maintain a positive self-image and strive to become the best that they can be through planned physical activities. From childhood through adulthood individuals are always developing their self-image and becoming the best that they can be. A child's self-perception begins in infancy through interaction with others. The ability to move effectively is closely associated with a child's self-perception. Because self-image has a direct bearing on one's ability and willingness to learn in any situation, the physical education curriculum must be carefully planned and implemented to help students learn to move effectively and efficiently, thereby enhancing a positive self-image and helping students to achieve their best. Students who lack appropriate movement skills may not feel good about themselves or about physical activity and will often choose not to be physically active. To realise their full potential through physical education, students should be encouraged to appraise their skills and talents realistically, make a personal commitment to a plan for improving those skills, take appropriate risks to achieve their goals, and persevere.

Growth and development

Children experience the stages of growth and development at different rates. When they learn that individuals are not automatically considered wrong or bad if they develop more slowly or more rapidly than their peers, they are better prepared to accept individual differences. At the same time certain aspects of physical development are relatively common at specific age and grade levels. An understanding of the body-type variations of endomorph, mesomorph, and ectomorph can help students accept capabilities and limitations that may be a function of body type. Therefore, an understanding of developmentally appropriate activities is necessary.

Psychology

Positive emotional development is closely related to good feelings resulting from movement in physical education activities. One aspect of positive emotional development is learning to acknowledge, accept, and appreciate differences between oneself and others with regard to abilities and achievement. Self-acceptance, which is enhanced as students take pride in personal excellence and try to improve their performance, is closely connected with developing a sense of personal responsibility. By overcoming physical challenges and other obstacles at each level of development, students acquire the confidence they need to progress further and to take on new challenges.

Curriculum Development

Staff can make physical education more accessible by helping pupils to participate at first hand. They can improve access by:

— using materials and resources that pupils can access through sight, touch, sound or smell, for example, different-sized, textured, noisy and fluorescent balls,

— using a range of activities where the first steps are for pupils to get involved, for example, in indoor and outdoor play, playground games, action songs and rhymes,

— making effective use of physiotherapy, occupational therapy, hydrotherapy and mobility programmes, designed to meet individual needs and promote access to a range of physical activities,

— ensuring pupils have first-hand and direct experiences in the different areas of activity of the national curriculum,

— ensuring consistent coactive support,

— making use of all appropriate available resources in the school, the local community and sporting organisations that can enhance the range of opportunities on offer to pupils, for example, sports centres and grounds, swimming pools and a range of other facilities, such as bowling, roller-skating or dry ski slopes,

- using ICT, visual and other materials, such as video or television, to increase pupils' knowledge of their personal surroundings and the wider world,
- using specialist aids, equipment and adapted workspaces to ensure the safe handling of tools, materials and equipment, for example, soft play area, adapted bikes, larger targets, shorter distances, balls with roughened surfaces,
- providing support from adults or other pupils when needed, but giving pupils space and freedom to do things for themselves and allowing pupils time to respond and use a range of equipment,
- providing alternative activities, where necessary, to overcome difficulties with manipulating tools, equipment or materials, for example, while some children may be able to explore whole body movements in the gym, some may need to explore them in the swimming pool where their bodies have greater freedom to move,
- taking account of the pace at which pupils work and of the physical effort required, and giving them time to be correctly positioned for the activity,
- ensuring a balance of consistency and challenge, according to individual needs.

Teaching physical education can help pupils develop their broader communication and literacy skills through encouraging interaction with other pupils as well as staff. With some pupils, communication and literacy skills will develop through using a range of visual, written and tactile materials, for example, large print, symbols and symbol text. These skills will also develop as pupils use

ICT and other technological aids. Other pupils' skills develop as they use alternative and augmentative communication, for example, body movements, eye gaze, facial expressions and gestures including pointing and signing.

When using the scheme of work, staff should:

— select a specific focus from the unit,
— make it relevant to pupils' experiences,
— identify clear expectations for pupils,
— reinforce and consolidate learning by repetition and variety.

The first and perhaps most important aspect of physical education is the direct bearing it has on children's physical, mental, and social wellbeing. The child who is well educated physically is likely to become a healthy adult who is motivated to remain healthy. Although adults are often well informed about health and pursue healthy lifestyles that include good nutrition, exercise, physical activity, and fitness, their children's physical health and well-being are frequently a cause for concern. Recognising the threat of a sedentary life-style inherent in postindustrial work patterns, large numbers of adults can be found jogging, walking, eating healthy foods, and seeking out ways to incorporate movement and activity into their daily routines. But at the same time alarming numbers of children and youths, often lacking appropriate adult supervision, can be found in front of television sets on sunny weekday afternoons munching on snack foods. This problem is compounded by approaches to physical education that have traditionally emphasized competition, games, sports, and native athletic ability, favouring those who are most talented and leaving the less able to view themselves as outsiders who will never make the grade. Our society can no longer afford that approach. A principal theme of this framework is that all children-regardless of disability, ethnicity, gender, native language, race, religion, or sexual orientation-must be given opportunities not only to succeed in physical education but to develop a lifelong commitment to the pleasure and the health benefits of physical activity.

A second reason for the importance of physical education today is its direct link with academic learning. The healthy, physically active child is more likely to be academically motivated, alert, and successful. In the preschool and primary years, there are direct links between active play, physical agility and coordination, and academic success. As children grow older and enter adolescence, healthy physical activity becomes integral to their self-concept and their ability to take on new intellectual, social, and emotional challenges. Throughout, physical education promotes the social skills and cooperation that are increasingly viewed by educators today as essential for success in school. Just as any well-planned academic curriculum takes into account a wide range of learning modes and styles, the physical education curriculum emphasizes a variety of cognitive, affective, and psychomotor teaching and learning strategies.

A physically educated person is one who has mastered the necessary movement skills to participate confidently in many different forms of physical activity, values physical fitness, and understands that both are intimately related to health and well-being. The most basic element of a child's development is learning to move. Even before birth children begin learning to move and learning through movement. The process continues throughout childhood and early adolescence. Movement skills are central to physical education at all grade levels.

Physical education addresses the child's fundamental need for regular physical activity to remain healthy and promotes many of the attitudes and behaviours that reduce health risks, including development of an understanding of the need for appropriate nutrition and exercise. A quality physical education programme can motivate students to maintain healthy eating habits and regular physical activity. A well-planned physical education programme guides students to becoming motivated to attain optimum health through regular use of new knowledge and skills. In a society that tends to be mechanised, stress-ridden, and sedentary, the physically educated person is prepared to participate throughout life in appropriate physical activities. He or she can also make choices that will minimise the risks of cardiovascular diseases that afflict one in four people in the United States. For the physically educated person, health and physical well-being are important personal values.

All children and youths need a well-planned physical education programme that begins at the earliest grade levels, receives strong support schoolwide, is understood and reinforced at home, and is supported by a comprehensive health education programme. All have the potential to achieve an active, healthy lifestyle. There are three major goals for the physical education curriculum. Supporting and reinforcing each of these goals are underlying disciplines. Throughout the kindergarten through grade twelve curriculum, all three goals of physical education are addressed, together with their respective disciplines. There is a flow of learning from one goal to another and from one grade level to another. Because movement and activity are central to physical education, the goal of movement skills and movement knowledge is the key to a well-planned programme. True comprehensiveness can be achieved, however, only through a focus on all three goals. Within each goal the appropriate disciplines support the knowledge, skills, and attitudes desired for every student. The disciplines are an important part of the knowledge base of physical education, guiding what is taught and when. They provide instructors with both a rationale for the instructional programme and specific content.

PERFORMANCE EVALUATION

Evaluating and improving performance begins with pupils being aware of what movements they can make, what they can achieve through those movements, and then tuning the movements and varying what they can do with them. Teaching this aspect across key stages can help pupils to:

- improve the quality of their own performance and presentation,
- develop their skills in communicating thoughts about an activity using their preferred mode of communication and appropriate vocabulary,
- develop their listening skills and the ability to collaborate with others and share ideas when exploring different options and possibilities,
- adapt and change actions and responses,
- become aware of the needs of others,
- improve their personal best and develop ideas further,
- recognise and cope with personal success and limitations,
- appreciate and acknowledge others' good work,
- explore and improve the quality of group work and the monitoring and recording of their own progress.

Knowledge and understanding of fitness and health begins with tolerating pain, maintaining good physical posture and correct positioning, and a willingness and desire to move and exercise. Teaching this aspect across key stages can help pupils to:

— become aware of the range of activities, including exercise and movement, necessary for their own health and personal wellbeing, for example, eating, sleeping, hygiene

— establish and develop positive attitudes to exercise and regularly take part in physical activity

— understand the importance of getting ready for, and recovering from, exercise and activity, for example, using repetitive warm up and cool down exercises, getting changed, washing.

Staff should be aware of, and carry out, risk assessments at regular intervals and make sure that pupils are engaged in appropriate activities and wear appropriate clothing.

6

Supportive Environment for Physical Education

A positive, supportive environment is important to the success of the overall physical education programme. Support for physical education should include the following elements:

— Physical education is recognised as an integral part of the school curriculum.

— Physical education continually supports and interacts with other subject areas.

— Physical education is included as part of a planned staff development programme.

— Facilities, equipment, and supplies are provided that are safe and adequate.

— The psychological environment enables and encourages all students to succeed in physical education.

— The physical education programme involves the school, the home, and the community.

As an integral part of the school curriculum, physical education should be taught by qualified professionals who have been trained in physical education or who have participated in a programme of professional development focusing on the teaching of physical education. Classes for children and youths with special needs or disabilities should be taught by physical education teachers who know how to design and implement programmes for such students. A quality physical education programme provides equal access for all students and guarantees opportunities for maximum participation, optimum development, and appropriate individual attention. Opportunities for personal attention, individualised instruction, and time on task should be included.

Physical education teachers should be encouraged to participate on school or district interdisciplinary teams to develop the physical education curriculum. In a well-planned programme the physical education teacher assumes responsibility for

(1) implementing the physical education curriculum;

(2) relating physical education to other subject areas;

(3) working with other professionals to create interdisciplinary approaches to learning; and

(4) promoting the cooperation of school, home, and community in providing the highest-quality physical education experience possible for every student.

Physical education should continually support and interact with the other subject areas. For example, in its emphasis on personal health and the need for a healthy lifestyle, physical education reinforces but does not supplant health education. Teachers of physical education and health education should work together to integrate their curricula to reinforce the importance of maintaining an active and healthy lifestyle. Both can emphasise skills related to refusing negative pressures and influences, resolving conflicts, and coping with pressure, all of which are necessary for positive social interaction and healthy development. Physical education classes provide a natural environment for the development of personal and social skills transferable to other situations and learning in other subject areas. There is a natural correlation, for example, between cooperative learning activities related to understanding the place of rules and strategies in physical education and the teaching of civic values, rights, and responsibilities in history-social science. Continual interaction should occur between teachers of physical education and the rest of the staff. Through this interaction physical education and the other disciplines support and reinforce one other. Other examples of integration with the rest of the curriculum include the following:

— *Natural sciences*-through concepts related to gravity, levers, motion, physics, anatomy, biomechanics, and exercise physiology

— *Home economics*-through the study of exercise physiology and nutrition

— *History-social science*-through an emphasis on guiding students to become active, productive members of a democratic society; work cooperatively in groups and teams; and develop an understanding of others through cross-cultural and multicultural games, dances, and other activities

— *English-language arts*-through applying physical education experiences in written assignments and other activities requiring communication skills

— *Mathematics*-through recording results and calculating probabilities, percentages, and averages related to physical activity or creating graphs to demonstrate measurements and comparisons of personal progress

— *Visual and performing arts*-through a shared emphasis on aesthetic perception, creative expression, rhythm, tempo, and meter

— *Career-vocational education*-through the study of careers in such areas as teaching, recreation, health, fitness, dance performance, and sports broadcasting

As emphasized throughout this framework, physical education includes more than the education of the physical body. All subject areas should function as integrated components in the education of the total individual.

Staff Development

A variety of staff development activities should be available to enhance the physical education programme. Teachers of physical education should be encouraged to

1) participate in ongoing staff development to improve instructional strategies and programme implementation;
2) remain current on educational research;
3) learn to be effective with an increasingly diverse student population; and
4) enjoy the benefits of working and learning with other professionals in the field.

They should also be encouraged to work with local colleges or universities to influence preservice training and provide in-service training opportunities.

At the school level physical education teachers should have opportunities to meet regularly with each other and with members of other departments or grade levels to assess the effectiveness of programmes and plan revisions. Ensuring compliance with state and federal mandates should be an important part of the assessment process as well. Teachers should be encouraged to become involved in professional organisations and contribute their expertise to staff development projects in physical education at the local, state, and national levels.

Indoor and Outdoor Facilities

Indoor and outdoor facilities must be sufficient in number, appropriate to the needs of all students, and accessible to the disabled. Dressing rooms must be clean and safe, adequate for the number of students served, and appropriately supervised without requiring physical education instructors to lose instructional time because of supervision. Equipment and supplies should be sufficient in quantity and quality to provide all students with opportunities to enjoy maximum participation. Safety is an important priority in the environment for a quality physical education programme. Staff members must be aware of safety concerns, protect students from unsafe equipment or facilities, and expect students to ensure their own safety and that of others. A student's lack of proficiency in English should not influence this priority in any way. Provisions should be made to ensure that all limited-Englishproficient students understand rules and expectations regarding safety. Others to be considered in ensuring the safety of all students should be persons with disabilities.

Psychological Environment

An appropriate environment for a quality physical education programme enables and encourages all students to discover new concepts, skills, and abilities through movement experiences and other aspects of the physical education programme. The atmosphere should be a nonthreatening one in which every student feels that to risk trying something new is safe physically, emotionally, and socially. Emphasis should be placed throughout on the development of movement skills, fitness and wellness, self-confidence, and social skills.

Because of the complexities of human growth and development and individual and cultural differences among students, a comprehensive physical education programme should include a wide variety of movement experiences and teaching-learning strategies. All students should have the opportunity to be successful. Throughout, the student must experience a climate of respect-for oneself, for others, and for physical education generally, especially when students are being directed in attempts to refine skills or are being disciplined. Disciplinary procedures should be appropriate to the infraction, and the assignment of physical exercise should not be used as punishment. To do so will not instill in the student a love of physical activity.

Another important aspect of the psychological environment is an emphasis on accepting and celebrating ethnic and cultural diversity, one of the most challenging issues in education. Physical education offers unique opportunities to bring students together in nonthreatening ways that emphasize fairness and cooperation. Because physical education involves students in working and playing together, students must be taught the personal and social skills, values, and attitudes needed for effective, positive social interaction. Disparaging remarks about an individual's disabilities, ethnicity, gender, native language, race, religion, or sexual orientation should not be tolerated. The physical education programme must comply fully with all federal and state mandates.

Appropriate instruction in physical education for culturally diverse populations may require special teaching skills and a focus on students' unique needs. Teachers must avoid cultural or gender biases and refrain from stereotyping students. Students from different cultures may respond differently to directions from the teacher, praise and acknowledgment from others, perceived expectations, and physical interaction. Teachers should learn to recognise and understand the influence of their students' cultural heritage and learn to accommodate diversity while achieving the goals of the physical education curriculum.

Learning Environment

Although the school is the primary learning environment for physical education, the home and community also play significant roles. Only through the cooperation of the school, the home, and the community can students become fully prepared for lifelong participation in physical activity and effective social interaction. The school site can become a focus for cooperation among families and outside support systems.

Designating the school as the contact point provides families with more opportunities to receive services that benefit the child's health and development. For example, interaction of school and family can help to promote an acceptance of physically active and healthier, happier, more productive lifestyles throughout the community. Schools can establish centers for wellness that provide assessment of physical well-being, individual counselling, and a variety of fitness activities. They can also involve families in other extracurricular activities at the school site and coordinate school and community recreational programmes.

The community, working closely with the school, can play an active role in promoting fitness and wellness by providing opportunities for physical activity for families and individuals. Through participation in a variety of physical activities at school, students will be better prepared to take advantage of opportunities for physical activity provided in the home or in the community.

Effective Instruction

This framework describes a comprehensive physical education system that will prepare young people for a lifelong commitment to physical activity, health, and well-being. To achieve this end, however, all students must be given sufficient opportunities to accomplish the physical education learning goals for each grade level. What is required is a comprehensive physical education system of high quality and consistency throughout the grade levels. Most important, it implies quality instruction and positive, productive interactions between teachers and students. To create high expectations for quality instruction, physical education teachers must continually strive to improve their effectiveness.

Teachers create an optimal learning environment and an effective learning experience for their students through careful planning. The heart of effective instruction is the actual physical education lesson. Throughout the lesson the teacher should maintain an orderly, safe, businesslike atmosphere and have clear expectations for the behaviour and achievement of students.

The teacher implements the lesson plan and makes adjustments as necessary for students not experiencing success or not participating. Each day should begin with a variety of warm-up exercises involving the muscles to be used in the instructional phase and lasting one or two minutes. All students should be expected to perform the exercises to the best of their ability. However, adjustments may need to be made to deal with individual abilities. The teacher supervises the students, explains the purpose of each exercise, and provides corrective or positive feedback.

Warm-up is followed by the instructional phase. At this point the teacher explains the purpose of the main activity, which will include demonstrations and explanations. Then comes the activity phase. During the activity phase each student is engaged in skill-learning time, with enough correct practice trials being provided during class time to acquire the desired skill. Activities should be designed to keep to a minimum the amount of time spent waiting in line and moving between activities. Equipment should be deployed efficiently.

Whenever possible, students should be placed in cooperative learning groups. When working with individual students, the teacher should personalise instruction by using the student's name and giving feedback equally to boys and girls and to high achievers and low achievers in appropriate ways. At the end of the class, the teacher should provide a chance for discussion or processing of the lesson, encouraging the students to review the objectives or key points. In this way students can see relationships, attitudes, values, and other insights related to the lesson, and teachers can adjust the lessons for optimal learning the next day.

Effective Instructional Strategies

Teachers should use a variety of teaching styles, including teacherdirected and student-initiated learning, to satisfy the learning styles of individual students and stimulate higher levels of thinking and creativity. Teaching styles might include command, practice, self-check, guided discovery, student-designed and student-initiated teaching, and selfteaching. Teachers should also employ a variety of instructional approaches, including competency-based learning, contract learning, drill, information processing, lecture, mastery learning, programmed instruction, and role-playing.

Especially appropriate for physical education instruction is cooperative learning. Assigning students to small learning groups (three to six members each) allows teachers and students to achieve a variety of goals, both social and cognitive. In addition, research has shown that cooperative learning produces higher achievement; improves cross-ethnic friendships and social skills; enhances self-image; and promotes greater interdependence, improved role-taking abilities (e.g., leadership), and a better classroom climate.

The first step in cooperative learning is the formation of heterogeneous teams. The size of each team will vary according to the activity; however, groups of three to six students (mixed as to ability, race, and gender) have proven to be most successful. After the teams have been formed, students need activities for team building and time to practice and receive feedback on appropriate social skills.

The specifics of cooperative learning lessons depend to a great extent on which method among many different cooperative learning approaches is chosen. However, the teacher must ensure positive interdependence and both individual and group rewards. A team can succeed only if all members are interdependent in their contributions toward a common goal.

Many types of instructional media and resources, as distinct from equipment for games and sports, are available to aid the physical education teacher. In addition to textbooks, workbooks, and more conventional printed materials, resources include films, filmstrips, videos, laser discs, CD-Rom, and large-screen projections of televised or videotaped images.

Physical education teachers should look for ways not only to incorporate a variety of instructional media into their teaching but also to make sure that the media are available and are included in the overall budget for physical education. Examples abound of appropriate instructional technology in physical education. Heart monitors can provide students with feedback on their heart rate while they are performing cardiovascular exercises. In addition, camcorders and video cameras can be used to capture students' performances for skill or strategy analysis. Computers can aid the teacher in the production of task cards or skill cards and can also be used to provide information and instructional modules to individuals or groups. When connected to laser disc players, videocassette players and other peripheral devices can capture students' interest through multimedia presentations.

A wide variety of computer software programmes are available that lead students through tutorials on various sport or fitness concepts, offering both instruction and assessment procedures. An interactive laser-disc system can present students with information generated by computer software linked to the laser-disc player at different points in the tutorial. The player, instructed by the computer software, displays the appropriate live-action example. Interactive programmes offer students a considerable amount of control over their own learning and the topics they wish to explore. Technology is also very useful in the assessment process.

Every physical education class includes students who are high achievers; those who are low achievers; and those, the majority, in the middle. Effective instructional strategies take into account the diverse needs of what are often very heterogeneous groups. All students, not just a select few, should receive positive feedback and reinforcement from the instructor or other students; and all should have opportunities to be involved.

All students, male and female, should be given the teacher's attention and feedback on an equal basis and should be called on equally to demonstrate new skills.

The teacher should also discipline males and females equally. Some students will come to physical education with motor or perceptual deficits; others, with more severe disabilities. Successful participation in physical activities by students with disabilities depends on the teacher's attitude and skill in providing instruction and support to all students. The teacher should continually encourage all students to learn and experience maximum enjoyment in physical education by understanding students' specific needs and encouraging students who are not disabled to accept and support those who are.

Children with disabilities, whether they are identified as needing special education and related services or not, have the right to a modification of the regular programme. In some instances an individualised education programme team at the school will determine that the appropriate least-restrictive environment for a physical education programme for students with disabilities is the general education class. To accommodate such students, the physical education instructor may have to make modifications and interventions.

In collaboration with the adapted physical education specialist, special education teachers, and ancillary personnel, the physical education teacher can modify instruction to accommodate students with disabilities without diminishing the value of the class for those without disabilities. Problem-solving skills and modified approaches to movement can be offered at the elementary level; flexible or optional unit schedules, at the middle or junior high school level; and elective or selective programmes, at the senior high school level. Teaching methods can be adapted to meet the needs of students through provision of a direct tutor, a buddy system that pairs students with disabilities with other students, peer tutoring, task cards or individualised learning packets, circuit or station setups, contracts or independent student programmes, and other approaches. Other adaptations might include:

- Basing evaluation on the student's potential and on pretest and posttest comparison rather than on standardised scores
- Basing measurement on what the student with disabilities is able to do rather than on what the student is not able to do
- Applying decathlon-scoring approaches to enable students with disabilities to compete for points against records that are appropriate to their physical status
- Providing specific devices or adapting equipment to aid in the manipulation of objects or oneself
- Using a larger ball or larger pieces of equipment to make the activity easier or to slow the pace of the activity
- Using a smaller, lighter ball or striking implement (plastic or soft ball or plastic bats) or an object that is easier to handle (beanbag or softball)
- Adding more players to a team to reduce the amount of activity and responsibility of any individual player
- Assigning playing positions according to the abilities of the students with disabilities
- Permitting the substitution or interchange of duties during participation
- Limiting play areas if students' movement capabilities are restricted

The physical education teacher should seek out opportunities for informal talks with the adapted physical education specialist or special education teacher to develop methods for working with students with disabilities. When these students cannot participate safely and successfully in the physical education programme and when interventions have been ineffective, the specialist in adapted physical education must take a more active role. Use of the individualised education plan process for special education may be required.

Different types of instructional approaches will also be needed for students with limited proficiency in English or other communication problems. Bilingual interpreters or instructors skilled in sign language may be needed. For non-English speakers, information offered in their native language helps develop not just understanding but a positive attitude toward the information. For teachers who do not speak a second language and for students who are limited-English proficient, sheltered instruction is another approach that can be used. Sheltered instruction provides students with a variety of interactive and multimodal means to accessing information.

In sheltered instruction the language demands of the lesson can be modified through such techniques as clear enunciation, controlled vocabulary, fewer idioms, and such contextual cues as gestures, facial expressions, demonstrations, props, visuals, and overhead transparencies. Cooperative learning has also proved effective in teaching students at various levels of English proficiency because high levels of interaction are associated with enhanced learning of content and English.

Instructional Resources

A basic physical education programme should include a description of the content of the resources as well as suggestions on how all students can be helped to gain access to that content and how the physical education teacher can be supported.

Instructional resources should reflect and support the vision, goals, and grade-level guidelines described in this framework. All the goals should be addressed, with support from their respective disciplines. Resources should present physical education as a comprehensive, sequential system that promotes the physical, mental, emotional, and social well-being of each student. The presentation of resources should be open and engaging, and vocabulary should be incorporated to facilitate understanding for both teachers and students.

Students should be encouraged to acquire understanding and knowledge about the content and skills of physical education. They should be able to grasp the why as well as the how of what they are doing. They should also understand that the content areas are vehicles for developing and refining skills. The content and skill areas are the basis of physical education. The idea of competition should be introduced gradually in instructional resources as in the overall physical education programme itself. Students should understand that competition equates with making the most of one's physical potential and capabilities in a positive, meaningful way.

Instructional resources in physical education should recognise cultural diversity and reflect strategies that research and practice have shown to be successful in engaging all students in learning. For all students to participate fully, tasks and activities should be made accessible to all students through a variety of approaches. Woven throughout, for example, should be a multicultural perspective promoting respect for the dignity and worth of all people regardless of their differences and building on the knowledge, attitudes, beliefs, and cultural and linguistic foundation that students bring to class. The instructional resources should include activities for all students, including students with disabilities.

Instructional guides should provide ways to make instruction for limited-English-proficient (LEP) students comprehensible, age-appropriate, and commensurate with their academic backgrounds. The provision of glossaries and summaries of key concepts in the students' primary language is one way of giving LEP students access to the physical education curriculum. The format of resources-including clear headings, subheadings, illustrations, photographs, graphs, and charts, all clearly labelled-can greatly increase the likelihood that all students will understand basic concepts. Such conventions are critical for students with special needs, such as LEP students.

Quality Assessment

Several different forms of assessment can be used to measure student progress and achievement in physical education: student portfolios, teacher observations, performance tests, open-ended questions, interviews, exhibitions, and cooperative group projects. The results of these assessments demonstrate how children use skills, solve movement problems, and progress over time. Assessment can also reveal the effectiveness of the instructional programme and provide insight into how physical education teachers can make learning more meaningful. Quality assessment informs students, teachers, and parents about each student's progress toward the yearly learning expectations. Student profile information should be documented and maintained to monitor students' progress from year to year. At the beginning of each term, the teacher should assess each student to determine appropriate student expectations, instructional starting points, and grouping approaches. However, the entire evaluation process should be viewed as a means rather than as an end.

Educators in all disciplines are moving increasingly toward authentic assessment, an evaluation process that can contribute to a lively, active, and exciting learning experience for students. Authentic assessment engages students in challenges requiring the application of skills, knowledge, and attitudes. It requires students to explain or demonstrate how they can use what they have learned.

The assessment, relevant feedback, and results are reported to each student immediately, together with a focus on the student's strengths and aspects of performance that may need improvement. Historically, physical education has always assessed fitness and motor skills. The challenge now is to find authentic assessment instruments for the cognitive and affective domains. Assessment in physical education should address the three major goals of physical education presented in this framework. A variety of methods can be used, including written tests; videotaped performances of skills; cooperative learning activities; individual, small-group, and class projects; problem-solving tasks; small-group and class discussions; task cards; work sheets; contracts; small-group and class projects; and homework.

Self-assessment is another means of providing students with information about their performance. Students can apply self-evaluation when given lists of performance objectives and directed to judge their own achievement. This procedure can be facilitated by the videotaping of the student's performance for follow-up viewing by the student. On a higher level self-assessment can offer opportunities for students to establish personal goals and make critical and valid evaluations as they monitor their progress. Establishing personal goals and practicing self-assessment should be an integral part of the students' learning experience in physical education. Self-assessment also helps motivate students to assume responsibility for their own learning.

Peer assessment, which can be carried out by learners in pairs or groups, is an effective evaluation method for sixth grade or above. As students develop peer assessment skills, they learn the importance of giving and receiving support and constructive feedback. In peer assessment the student evaluator compares and contrasts another student's performance with the criteria established by the teacher. The results can be communicated orally or through the use of a task card, rating scale, or checklist. Peer assessment can be done live or can be videotaped.

Grades should bear a close relationship to the course goals and learning expectations. Course grades should not be used to report such elements as attendance, cleanliness, personality, punctuality, and wearing apparel. Assessment should require students to:

— Demonstrate an understanding of the application of information in new and familiar tasks.

— Explain why and how rather than merely perform movement.

— Integrate and connect understanding, analyse self-performances, observe others, and experiment with this knowledge.

— Demonstrate imagination, persistence, and creativity and show a capability for problem solving.

The physical education grade, based on the individual's progress toward the course objectives, should be included in the high school grade point average along with all other grades and should be accepted by colleges and universities. Grading based on the achievement of clearly stated goals and objectives emphasizes what students know and can do. One form of grading involves an assessment instrument that describes a standard against which a piece of work or skill is judged. The assessment instrument tells the student what has to be accomplished. For the evaluation to be valid and fair, the student and evaluator must share a common understanding of what is to be accomplished. Throughout the semester students should be kept informed of their grades. Before any evaluation they should be provided with enough time for instruction and practice.

7

Assessment of Physical Fitness Training

Definitions and performance standards of physical fitness vary. However, most experts agree that the five basic components of fitness are:

1. *Cardiorespiratory or Aerobic Endurance.* The ability to do moderately strenuous activity over a period of time. It reflects how well your heart and lungs work together to supply oxygen to your body during exertion and exercise. Also called aerobic fitness.
2. *Muscular Endurance.* The ability to hold a particular position for a sustained period of time or repeat a movement many times. This could be the capability required to hold a two-pound weight above your head for five minutes or the effort required to lift that weight 20 consecutive times.
3. *Muscular Strength.* The ability to exert maximum force, such as lifting the heaviest weight you can budge, one time. It is possible to have muscular strength in one area, say your arms, while lacking strength in another area such as your legs.
4. *Flexibility.* The ability to move a joint through its full range of motion; the elasticity of the muscle. This is how limber or supple you are.

5. *Body Composition*. The proportion of fat in your body compared to your bone and muscle. It does not refer to your weight in pounds or your figure.

Physical fitness is affected favourably or unfavourably by the influences which contribute to, or detract from, all of the functioning parts of the organism and the organism as a whole. To attain and maintain fitness, one must live the intelligent life, making constant adjustments to one's environment and accepting the responsibility of changing it when such change is needed. This means a rational programme of activity, an adequate and balanced diet, ability to control psychological and physical stimuli and to resolve the resultant stress that they cause, prompt and competent medical care, and, of course, a sound philosophical basis for coping with contingencies for which no planning can be made. In short, the intelligent life means rational judgements tempered with human emotional overtones which add both spice and grandeur.

Physical education is generally concerned with specific aspects of fitness dealing with physiologic competence. This is not to indicate that such concern can be placed in a vacuum called "physical" or "the body" and be treated in isolation from the whole. But it does imply that physical educators mainly and by tradition use as their tool for total fitness the neuromuscular aspects of man and attempt to condition him though activity for the stress he will inevitably meet. Physical education's concern with fitness is functional rather than anatomical, although both areas are interrelated. Our scientists, philosophers, holists, educators, better-informed physical educators, and even our poets have pro-claimed that there is more to fitness than muscle strength. A conference of such people described fitness as "that state which characterizes the degree to which the person is able to function." This implies the ability of each person to develop his potentialities most effectively. In addition, the conference agreed that fitness is maintained at a high level only if motivation is continuously present! An inner desire is required; the activities which produce fitness must have meaning.

We will define physical fitness as a fitness to perform some specified task requiring muscular effort. It is evident that since muscular effort may be evaluated in terms of strength, speed and endurance, these may be the various aspects of fitness. Although the term physical fitness has a questionable connotation, numerous attempts have been made to evaluate "the functional capacity for the task". Both muscular performance and organic function have been used as criteria for measuring fitness. Obviously, anatomical fitness, meaning possession of all the parts and organs of the body which are necessary for the task, is basic.

Physiological fitness means skillful performance and rapid recovery, and psychological fitness implies emotional stability, drive, intelligence, motivation, and educability. Ideally, a fitness test should take into account all of these aspects of fitness. Lacking such, people have had to assess themselves against standards of so-called normal structure, control, and psychological elements in approaches to tasks, and then to measure how much work a person can do in a limited time and observe what happens to the body during and after the task.

The fit man usually shows the following physiological advantages over the unfit man of the same height and weight when both are performing the same piece of moderate work which both can sustain in a steady state: lower oxygen consumption, slower pulse rate during work, larger stroke volume of the heart, lower blood lactate during work, and faster return of blood pressure and heart rate to normal after work. If both a fit and an unfit man are performing the same piece of exhausting work which neither can sustain in a steady state, the fit man usually shows longer duration of effort before exhaustion, higher oxygen consumption, slower maximal heart rate, larger stroke volume, higher blood lactate and faster return of blood pressure and heart rate to normal after work. Since there is always a syndromic reaction to an exercise bout in terms of cardiorespiratory function, a relatively accurate measure of functional fitness can be obtained by evaluating the response of a single factor.

Post exercise heart rate has been used most often to measure this particular syndrome and hence to measure functional fitness. One of the most valid. reliable, and easy to administer tests of physical fitness in terms of heart recovery rate is the Harvard fatigue Laboratory Test of Physical Fitness, usually referred to as the Harvard Step Test. It appears that "physical" fitness can be maintained only be continuing to train muscularly at atleast a minimal level. There is no "easy" way to fitness. Lying on a vibrating couch, being massaged, or riding an electrically driven bike, will do little to maintain physical condition. Active, dynamic exercise is the only way to organic efficiency. Such exercise results is strength, agility, flexibility, coordination, and ultimately endurance.

Physical fitness programmes rely heavily upon running, vigorous sports, and gymnastics, for fitness is a "do-it-yourself" matter. Functional integrity and well-being are achieved only as one remains active. Fitness can be lost as quickly as it is gained. The current way of life in the United States does a great deal to discourage organic fitness on the part of children as well as adults. The rubber tire has replaced shoe leather electronic conveniences have replaced shoulder girdle muscles, and a life of non-movement has replaced the vigorous activity of the past. It seems quite feasible that those who have matured in a world which does not encourage gross body movement will have to pay the penalty in terms of weakness and softness. Obviously, there is no standard fitness for all; fitness is "neither a fixed standard nor an average, but rather an objective," It varies according to sex, occupation, hereditary pattern, and level of interest. What is fitness for one may well be softness for another.

Physical education has the unique opportunity to help people attain an organic well-being through activity—an opportunity that no other discipline has. Physical educators would be less than true to their heritage and would be ignoring their responsibility if they did not consider such fitness as essential by-product of their particular programme. However, let it be noted that the intelligent physical educator should be discreet in his enthusiasm for a "unique contribution" for there is real danger in equating physical education with physical fitness alone. The two are not interchargeable terms in spite of the fact that total fitness is one of the basic aims of all education.

Acquiring Physical Fitness

Physical fitness is acquired by undertaking a specified amount of physiological work which must be continually increased in terms of resistance and speed. Only through overload can the body be adequately conditioned. If training is systematic. Certain specific results may be anticipated: there will be systemic change in the body an functional change in individual reaction.

Respiration Control

Usually, oxygen is more readily available to the blood; the trained person seems to need less air than the untrained. The minute volume of the person who is trained has a tendency to decrease while the oxygen absorption tends to increase. The endurance of the respiratory muscles is raised, so that the discomfort of chest restriction felt during exercise is reduced. Alveolar tissue tends to form new elements. There is a marked hypertrophy of the diaphragm muscle. Each of these respiratory adjustments makes the respiratory system more efficient. Since there seems to be evidence that respiration is the keystone to endurance, efficient respiratory patterns are an essential aspect of total fitness. It should also be noted that the lungs cannot store oxygen, and the use of oxygen by athletes has no known physiological advantage.

The circulatory system is dramatically influenced by exercise. The capillaries in the active muscles multiply, allowing the muscles to have a larger blood supply. Capillary increase takes place not only in the active muscle tissue but in heart muscle and in the motor area of the cerebral cortex. All of this enriches the circulatory process and contributes to the efficiency of the total person. Severe and persistent training results in hypertrophy of the heart beyond the limits usually acknowledged as normal. There is nothing alarming about this enlargement.

The term which is sometimes applied to it, athlete's heart, is to be valued rather than feared. Like any other muscle, the heart gets larger through exercise, and this hypertrophy has organic integrity. It is a normal result of intense activity. Heart size is related to thoracic circumference as well as hereditary factors.There seems to be a tendency for sports which require long endurance to enlarge the right side of the heart, while intensive brief exertion produces its greatest change on the left side of the heart.

With training there is a reduction in the heart rate. The heart beats more slowly but more powerfully. The increased stroke volume offsets the decreased heart rate so that really more blood is sent out with each stroke. As a result of the greater minute volume, the heart is able to pump larger amounts of blood to the active muscles during exercise and so permit more muscular endurance. During exercise it is possible for the minute volume of the blood to increase as much as ten times.

Exercise raises the velocity of circulation flow through cardiac adjustment and skeletal muscle contraction. During training, systolic blood pressure has a disposition to rise; increased diastolic pressure after exertion is the usual systemic identification of many conditioned athletes. the frequency of heart rate during exercise bouts is a linear relationship with the work load: the heavier the load, the harder the heart must work. The only exception to this rule occurs when the physiological work load calls for a sustained contraction such as the press in weight lifting. This contraction has a tendency to hinder the return of the venous blood to the heart. Holding the breath, which usually accompanied sustained contraction, increases intrathoratic pressure and thus also inhibits venous return. As a result of training, the heart returns to its homeostatic level more quickly after exercise.

The heart rate is governed by a small node of very specialized muscle, the sinoauricular node or the "pacemaker," which discharges the rhythmic impulses initiating the heartbeat. The nerves supplying the heart are autonomic and are classified as the vagus nerve and the sympathetic nerves. The slow rate of the trained person is due to what may be described as increased vagal tone. Emotional states cause a stress syndrome which characteristically increases the heartbeat. This psychic response is usually evident in the first few minutes of exercise and may even be manifested as a result of anticipation of exercise. It is not known whether this reaction is caused by adrenal secretion or not, but it can be surmised that the physical and emotional stress in exercise augments the heart rate.

Therefore, athletes who are anticipating play are quite normal in having a faster pulse rate. In addition, there is evidence to indicate that carbon dioxide and temperature can change heart rate, as does a change in the blood oxygen content. At any rate, the trained individual appears to have a greater capacity to endure the discomfort of some of these cardiac changes than does the untrained individual. Also many of these cardiac changes seem to facilitate oxygen transport, which is absolutely essential to the endurance of any working muscle.

Changes in Blood Chemistry

The blood chemistry undergoes some rather interesting changes as a result of training and conditioning. There is some controversy as to whether the alkaline reserve is increased, but certainly the rate of lactic acid formation is reduced; thus the blood lactate concentration is lower in the trained than in the untrained. During exhausting exercise bouts, the former seems to be able to tolerate higher lactate concentration in the blood than the latter. This toleration seems to have a relationship to endurance. Under certain conditions of very intense work, some of the lactic acid that enters the bloodstream is eliminated by the kidneys, and it is possible to find sodium lactate in the urine for some time after exercise. Training increases the red blood corpuscle count—the red bone marrow becomes redder.

Prolonged, extensive muscular effort can cause the destruction of red blood corpuscles to the point of anemia, but usually the red bone marrow is so developed during training that any normal destruction of red blood corpuscles is corrected. The white blood cells do not seem to be affected by training, although there is a decrease of eosinophils, which are leucocytes, as a result of the stressors of activity and activity anticipation. The specific gravity of the blood has a direct correlation with the erythrocyte picture. It increases during periods of exercise, then drops below normal immediately following the work, only to rise to its homeostatic level again. Various trials of moderate exercise do not have a pronounced effect on the blood sugar, but if there is great emotional involvement or the trial is particularly strenuous, the blood sugar does rise. When the exercise is prolonged, the blood sugar has a tendency to drop. There are some reasons to believe that level of blood sugar has some effect on endurance; the closer to normal the blood sugar level the better the individual's condition. However, blood sugar cannot be augmented instantly, and the use of honey and sugar immediately before or during a game is questionable. In general, a fitness programme does not cause drastic changes in blood chemistry, but training does appear to increase tolerance for any blood changes there are.

Improvemet of Musculature

It is thought that the number of muscle fibres does not increase as a result of training, although each fibre may hypertrophy. In addition, the fit individual gains in muscular strength and endurance: his phosphocreatine content rises, and the active muscles maintain a very red colour, probably due to increased hemoglobin content. This improved transportation of blood to the muscles undoubtedly facilitates the gain in endurance. Consequently, as man gets stronger he can do more and thus continue to increase his strength.

Improvement of Nervous System

The improvement in skill patterns of the trained individual argues well for some essential change in the central nervous system. It has been suggested that the transmission of the nervous impulse over the motor end plate is aided by training, also that the chemical mediums at the synapses change to improve nervous response. If such is true, it might explain why it is possible to improve coordination and to change reaction time to a certain extent. Although only certain muscles are used in any one specific exercise, the entire body responds via the nervous system. Thus, the tonic neck reflex is employed in exercise demanding all-out hand grip effort. In fact, many of the muscular mannerisms employed by athletes under great strain are probably really "assists" given via the central nervous system to facilitate the task at hand. There seems to be just reason for facial grimaces during certain exercises of exertion, and the trained individual employs these extraneous actions frequently.

Good Digestion

Exercise has little influence on the digestive ability of the organism. However, intense and prolonged exercise does temporarily inhibit gastric acid secretion and peristalsis. This inhibition often causes one to feel as if he had "lead in his stomach" and may well have contributed to the time-honoured rule that there shall be no swimming until one hour after a meal. Stomach distention may interfere with diaphragmatic breathing and this cold certainly affect exercise. Training does not "improve" one's digestion except as the abdominal muscular action assists in normal peristalsis. Conditioning is important to fitness. If the conditioning is regular and systematic, utilizing the principle of overloading to insure maximum effort, the following results should take place in reference to the systemic function of the organism:

— Breathing will become slower and deeper, thus enabling the athlete to undertake more work without being winded.

- The increase in capillaries and greater availability of oxygen will make the athlete less susceptible to muscular fatigue.
- Greater mechanical efficiency, resulting from cardiorespiratory adjustments, will increase the participant's endurance.
- There will be a circulatory adjustment with a lower heart rate and larger stroke-volume. This will permit strenuous exercise without throbbing and palpitation of the heart.
- There will be a more rapid return of the heart rate and blood pressure to their homeostatic levels, which will speed up the athlete's recovery from fatigue and quickly ready him for subsequent play.
- Adjustment in the blood chemistry will allow the individual to tolerate greater amounts of lactate in the blood and thus to withstand fatigue better.
- There will be improved muscle tone, resulting in greater muscular strength and endurance.
- Some muscular hypertrophy will occur as a result of muscular contraction.
- There will be an improvement in skill patterns with resulting neuromuscular facilitation; consequently, techniques will become easier as they are practiced.

FATIGUE AND PHYSICAL TRAINING

Fatigue is a natural condition. It was once described as being caused principally by the lactic acid produced by muscular contraction. However, such a simple explanation is inadequate, for fatigue is a very complicated phenomenon. It is now thought the organism never really reaches a point of complete fatigue, a point which would herald true exhaustion. If such were possible, a fatigued heart or diaphragm would be unable to function and death would follow. General fatigue is now believed to have a neurological origin, psychic as well as physical. Fatigue is signaled by diminished capacity for doing an assigned task effectively, local tiredness in specific music groups, a general feeling of tiredness throughout the entire body, sleepiness, localized, pain, soreness, stiffness and swelling inability to concentrate and recall, and slowness of comprehension. All of these symptoms usually are subjectively interpreted, so that fatigue is almost unmeasurable. Indeed, it can really be measured only in terms of changed performance. It seems apparent that if all else has been kept constant, fatigue is the most important factor in causing performance change.

In physical education classes, fatigue may be identified in a number of ways. The unskilled student who cannot keep up with the class in the gymnasium develops tiredness and asks to be excused. This fatigue may become chronic, a condition that will be identified with the experience; that is, the very thought of physical education will have the power to make him tired. Or fatigue may be manifested in a state of anxiety by the highly nervous athlete who uses up his energy in his pre-game practice and has nothing left for the playing situation. Or fatigue may taken the form of boredom; standing in the goalie cage, for example, waiting for the ball that never comes, may bring on fatigue that is psychically induced.

The most usual type of fatigue, however, is that found on the gymnasium floor after the basketball game, on the playing field after hockey or football, on the tennis court after the last set or the golf course after the last hole. The player has given his all and is sufficiently exhausted so that he would find it difficult to continue with the activity. Although each of these states of fatigue apparently is brought about by differing circumstances, there is a great deal of similarity in the end result. Boredom, staleness, anxiety, and muscular work create the sensation and it is that sensation which the physical educator must attempt to understand.

Fatigue should not be thought of as a purely physical and metabolic state. Of course, muscular work will increase the output of lactic acid, which in turn may adversely affect the end organs of the nerves, which in turn may become less efficient in their operation. But such a physical syndrome is only part of the story. Inability to function is not a simple thing and the psychic evertones are tremendous. A feeling of fatigue may stem from a variety of cause besides muscular work. The individual is a whole, and the fatigue can be due to both physical and psychic factors—each dependent upon the other.

There is a real difference between actual impairment and a feeling of tiredness. In the former, the vital activities of the cells are weakened, sometimes thwarted entirely, by the poisonous end products of the activity, which interfere with the normal function of the muscle cells. Such impairment can be relieved only by rest, sleep or at least a lessening of activity.

Fatigue may be a part of the general reaction to any stimulus or stressor agent. Possibly fatigue, or an impression of fatigue, alerts the individual to the stressful situation. Then, as the homeostatic level is again reached by resolution of the stressor, fatigue is relieved. Thus, fatigue may be a symptom of homeostatic upset as well as its result.

"Staleness" among athletes may be largely psychological. The performers may be bored with drill, practice, and the discipline of the training routine. The players exhibit their boredom in weariness, lack of snap, loss of interest, what seems to be lack of endurance, and a disposition toward accidents. This behavior may be due to fatigue induced by boredom: usually it can be alleviated by introducing novelty into practice sessions, by introducing the aspect of fun, and by attempting to remove some of the constant pressures of practice and substituting new, challenging, and untried pressures. There are even times when a day off from practice can do wonders. Frequently the joy, satisfaction, and sense of achievement inherent in sports success are effective antidotes to the fatigue generated by the frustrations of life itself. Over and over it has been observed that men who are employed on manual jobs involving heavy labour find their recreation at the end of the day in such physical activity as a game.

Some activities produce only moderate fatigue, but in sufficient quantities to be felt. Sitting all day at a desk, standing at a bank window, working over a steam table, selling clothes, checking out groceries in the local supermaker—all these may produce weariness from boredom or from an accumulation of lactic acid and other fatigue products at the distal parts. There has usually not been enough gross physical activity to facilitate the removal of the fatigue products, just enough to produce them. Often, activity involving large muscle action is the best counterbalance. In other words, general fatigue tends to dissipate the products and thus relieve local fatigue.

Fatigue is less likely to develop if one is engaged in something interesting. If the meaning and value of a task are kept clearly in mind, the entire enterprise is absorbing and socially and psychologically welcome. If there are rewards in status, social approval, or esteem, fatigue is less likely to occur. Conversely, excessive tiredness accompanies the enterprise that is distasteful, unrewarding, or socially unacceptable. It is easy to become tired even at the thought of doing some things; and when tiredness is present, it is difficult to simulate enthusiasm. Too often, this is the picture presented by the teacher: fatigued by papers, meetings, lessons, and discipline, and feeling that the rewards of the job are meager. Sometimes this fatigue can be ameliorated by looking at the job through different eyes. There seems to be some virtue in occasionally donning rose-coloured glasses.

The physical education teacher need be concerned less about fatigue if the games, aquatics, dance, and sports offered are rewarding and challenging. The fatigue factôrs operate in the long seasons of training which are typical of football and basketball. Long seasons and long practice sessions are frequently self-destructive, and their monotony has turned many a player away from further association with the game. The same danger is prevalent in pushing highly organized games down further in the elementary grades. Many potentially good players are sick of the game before they reach the stage where their skills are really good. Early chronic fatigue is one of the hazards of junior high and elementary school competitive sport. On the other hand, it is essential that these age groups be challenged by activity that it is not boring. Young children are ready for games of intrigue and skill and these need not be the same games that are played at the high school and college level.

It is possible for the individual, under emotional stress, to expend tremendous amounts of energy without feeling any marked degree of fatigue. The situation must be dealt with in a unitary way. Hormonal stimulation often obliterates the fatigue feeling and work results are phenomenal. This accounts for the effect that a contest has on "pepping up" a team. The relationship of ideas to harmone secretion is very real, and there is reason to believe that the body experiences greater stress from psychic than from physical influences. In moments of emergency one can play with abandon and force, "over his head," as it were. He becomes so enthusiastic and absorbed in what he is doing, his motives are so powerful, that all else becomes secondary and be responds with all out endeavour.

Motivation tempers fatigue and should be used to reduce fatigue caused by boredom or insecurity. It has been demonstrated experimentally that motivation delays the onset of fatigue and encourages greater work output. The physical education teacher, though making use of this knowledge, should not that there is some danger in increasing work output. If an individual is so powerfully motivated that he does not recognize or heed the ordinary signs of fatigue, impairment may take place. The wise teacher will utilize motivation up to a certain point but will recognize the fine dividing line when it is apparent that additional motivation may do more harm than good.

Frequent and intense periods of work with adequate rest between them are to be preferred to sustained work with little rest. It is much wiser to hold a practice for fifteen minutes three times during the hour, with five-minute breaks between periods, than to attempt to hold an hour's drill with no break. It is suggested that a rest period of at least 45 minutes be provided between strenuous events, especially those that are based upon speed, like swimming events or running races in track. Rest is best accomplished in a horizontal position, with the legs elevated. If it is not possible to lie down, mild exercise is better than inactivity. It is better to walk about than to stand or sit.

Fatigue is neither simple nor well understood. Its relation to nutritional states, vision, climatic conditions, variations in grandular secretions, emotionality, sleep, auditory stimuli, and many other factors needs further explanation. Indications are that the capacity for movement will loom larger, not as productive of fatigue, but as the antidote for it, in a modern world which seems predisposed to fatigue. It is not unreasonable to believe that the weariness and boredom which appear to affect many today can be alleviated by physical activity. Teachers must impart those skills in school which will later be used as preventives of fatigue.

Developing Strength

Muscular strength is a mark of muscular development and muscular development come through activity—in work and play. The strength which accrues through work and play must be neither so little as to be futile nor so much as to be superfluous. There is no completely objective measurement of the strength needed for any aspect of living. Measurement is only in terms of function, efficiency, and well-being. To ignore the value of muscular strength on the grounds that it is "physical" and hence of a lower order than "mental" or "spiritual" is educationally attenable. Strength is needed for specific purposes. The jumper needs powerful legs, the house painter needs strong shoulder girdle development, the mason needs a strong back. There are two ways to develop such strength; by taking special exercises or by working. Once the specific strength is achieved and the individual is satisfactorily meeting the demands of the job, he should refrain from the illogical assumption that because a particular strength is good for him it is good for everyone.

It is necessary to distinguish between the strength required for general well-being and the strength required for specific purposes. Muscle strength is needed by all to some degree, but in widely varying amounts. Arthur Steinhaus has remarked. Is strength a desirable goal? Does modern man need large muscles? Let us assume that you weigh 160 pounds; 64 pounds or about 40 per cent of this weight is in muscle. In other words, you have a 64 pound motor whose function is to support, move and transport this total of 160 pounds of body. Depending on your occupation, this motor must, in addition, do more, or less external work, as, for example, shovelling coal, digging a garden, stoking a furnace, or changing an automobile tire. The ideal muscular equipment is that which has just enough margin of strength or power to maintain posture without effort, to do the day's work easily, and to handle one's body weight readily. Beyond this point, it is wise to observe the maxims: "Truck-horse muscles are out of place on a buggy-horse job," and "Why bang around with a five ton truck when a run-about will do?" Only under extreme conditions of paralysis and death does a muscle become wholly relaxed or stretched to its full length. Most of the time it is in a state of partial contraction called tonus. Tonus permits the muscle to spiring into action smoothly.

The better the general condition of the organism, the better the tonus, the more efficient a machine the organism is at work and play. If tonus were lacking, every movement would require the inertia of a completely limp muscle to be overcome, and the amount of energy necessary for that task would appreciably increase the total energy output for all work. Tonus can vary as a result of weariness, sickness, lack of muscular activity, psychological duress, and other causes. When there is a lack of tone, tendons and ligaments are more prone to injury. This is well recognized in middle-aged persons who have been leading a sedentary life.

When a sudden demand is made upon their musculature such as raising a child from his crib, swinging a club on the weekend golf party, running a race at the office picnic, refinishing a "do-it-yourself" basement, or snatching up a heavy suit-case, things for which they are ill prepared, the whole force of the task is taken upon the tendons or ligaments rather than the resilient muscle. the result is sprains, strains, "sacroiliacs", wrenched backs, and even herniated disks in the spinal column. The veritable epidemic of such injuries in middle age can be traced largely to the effect of the sedentary life upon the muscle tissue. Strength and tonus decrease; the muscle is less able to stand sudden or prolonged activity. To copy with this situation one must remain active. There is less chance of injury if the muscles are kept reasonably strong through work and play and if muscular tonus is sustained. There is no substitute for self-initiated activity in this connection. One cannot wish himself strong; he must work for strength by active participation. In the judgement of many people, the key to the entire problem of muscular strength is in the abdominal wall. They feel that if the strength and tone of the abdominal muscles are maintained, many other muscular considerations will take care of themselves. There is some merit to such claims.

The abdominal muscles are very important in maintaining the normal position of the viscera. If the muscles are weakened, the weight of the viscera will respond to gravity and force the abdominal wall outward, encouraging a "bay window" contour. If the muscles remain strong, this is less likely to happen. In addition, the abdominal muscles are central and are involved in almost all activities that call for total body participation. When the trunk is active, the entire body benefits and the abdominal wall is the obvious target. Peripheral exercise is necessary to strengthen the arms and legs, but even with peripheral exercise the central trunk is very often involved. Endurance is related to and partially contingent upon strength. Endurance is thought of as a sustained effort to act effectively under the strain of a given task. The ability to endure often involves the ability to withstand the effects of fatigue and to develop a threshold of fatigue which is high enough to insure the completion of the task and the well-being of the participant. An interesting observation was made not long ago by one of the instructors at a national service academy. He remarked that although men were entering the services with more physical skills than they had ever before evidenced, they were also arriving with a great deal less endurance—so much less that it was affecting their ability to complete tasks.

Only as strength is developed can endurance be obtained. Endurance depends upon cardiac efficiency, respiratory efficiency, and muscular efficiency, and each of these systems is improved through exercise and its ultimate product—fitness. The psychic inhibitions to endurance are many, and if some of these can be removed, the resulting strength and endurance are astonishing. To make a man believe that he can win may provide the necessary spurt that assures his peak performance.

Weight Control

For many years it was thought that exercise did little to control weight. Detailed and extensive tables were drawn up of the calorie expenditure required of various activities and these figures were then compared to the expenditure of energy necessary to burn up one pound of fat. From the figures, it was estimated that to lose one pound of fat an individual would have to walk about 35 miles, split wood for 7 hours, or participate in a game such as basketball for 4 hours. Such figures were discouraging, to say the least, and the majority of nutritionists thought that diet control was the only way to regulate weight. It was also assumed that an increase in physical activity was always followed by an increased appetite. Therefore, exercise was actually discouraged in relation to weight control. Today, we know that these assumption represent only a partial truth. The dietary allowance varies from 1500 to 1600 calories per day and is contingent on the age, height, weight, sex and occupation of the individual. The sedentary female secretary may require but 1800 calories per day, while the trackmen, who is in training and is running at least 2 hours each day, may have a caloric requirement of 5000 calories. Just to be a functioning human being takes a certain number of calories, which are used to maintain the basic metabolic rate. More calories are needed for any activities which require an energy expenditure. Sitting, walking more than standing, and so on. Efficiently calls for the expenditure of energy. In addition, it takes greater energy to move greater poundage, and the energy cost of any exercise is proportional to the body weight. Thus, the overweight individual requires more energy expenditure for the same amount of exercise than would his slimmer counterpart.

Overweight may be more closely related to inactivity than food intake. Inactivity seems to augment the appetite even more than does a programme of activity. The reason for this is not really clear; undoubtedly it has a psychological rather than a physiological basis. Also of interest is the fact that intense activity tends to reduce the appetite temporarily. Many athletes have been unable to eat immediately after hard-fought contest. In addition, emotional excitation also may act as a deterrent to the appetite as seen in the appetite loss experienced by may players before a game. In a recent study comparing "active" and inactive" high school girls, the non-obese were found to be much more active than the obese, in spite of the fact that the caloric intake was usually larger in the non-obese than the obese since the fat individual needs more food to maintain herself.

More and more nutritionists are becoming convinced that inactivity is the single most important factor in the problem of "creeping" overweight in many modern

Western societies. Mayer suggests that the only way for the individual to control weight realistically in our society is to step up his activity pattern or be mildly to acutely hungry most of the time. Mayer strongly recommends that "a reorganization of one's life to include regular exercise adapted to one's physical potentialities is a justified return to the wisdom of the ages." It is the physical education teacher's responsibility to see that no one is excused from class on account of obesity. On the contrary, a real effort should be made to encourage the active participation of all obese individuals. Too often the fat girl or the fat boy becomes the goalie, the fullback in soccer, the center in football, the net man in badminton. The activity called for in these positions does not exact an energy expenditure which is justifiable in terms of weight control. Body weight can often be maintained by reasonable amounts of daily exercise and a small reduction in caloric intake.

The additional poundage accumulated over a span of years is usually due to reduced activity and expanded food intake, in terms of calories. If the opposite routine should be encouraged, that is, if physical activity were expanded, and food intake were reduced slightly, or at least held steady, it would appear that weight could be controlled. This is certainly one of the objectives of physical education.

There is no reason to believe that the physical fit individual is any more immune to bacteria and virus infection than the one who is not fit. We frequently speak of increasing individual resistance by exercise, fresh air, good food and rest. All of these measures are important for the maintenance of health but they do not afford protection against communicable diseases. An athlete in the best of health is just as susceptible to measles, smallpox or scarlet fever as in his friend who leads a sedentary life." Surely, there is a paucity of evidence to show a positive and direct relationship between exercise and an increase in the antibodies of the bloodstream. As long as resistance depends upon antigen-antibody relationship specifically and not upon general buildup, little can be said which argues a favorable effect of exercise upon resistance. However, general well-being apparently does make one better able to combat pathogens after they have attacked. A strong heart can be helpful during periods of illness. The improved venous and lymph circulation which results from activity and well-being may aid in the elimination of toxic products, and the ability to withstand fatigue and the fatigue products undoubtedly abets the body in its battle against exposure and illness.

STRESS CONTROL

The stress has three phases. The body is first made aware of the stressor on stimulus which is impinging upon it by means of the alarm reaction stage. In this stage, the body alerts itself to the stressor via the endocrine, circulatory, and the nervous systems. If the stressor persists, the body enters the stage of resistance, during which the individual attempts to resolve the stressor by adrenal-cortical secretions which combat or isolate the stressor agents. If resolution is not successful and the stressor continues, the body enters the stage of exhaustion which may precede death. Stress may be brought on by physical, chemical, and psychological stressors, and there is reason to believe that the psychological stressors have great potency. Since activity can inflict stress upon the body via physical stressors, it stands to reason that movement, by and of itself, is a stressor. In addition, physical education activities usually involve some psychological element and so intensify the stressors which impinge upon the body in even the mildest game situation. It would appear therefore that games should be avoided so that stress can be avoided. But such is not the case. A full life is a stressful life, and lack of movement is probably the most destructive stressor of all. In addition, gross body movement apparently has the ability to dissipate the products of stress just as it dissipates the products of fatigue, and activity may act as a tranquilizer. The relationship of physical education activities to stress and its general adaption syndrome is just beginning to be explored.

The interest of physical education in posture is historic. People have been concerned about posture for generations and it has been assumed that one of physical education's main purposes is to improve had posture and to correct poor posture. The muscles and ligaments of the body have been just pliable enough in a sufficient number of instances to give credence to this possibility. Recent thinking and experimentation have altered some of the early ideas. Bruce L. Bennett remarks, "Although there are some who believe that poor posture is the cause of many ailments such as backache, constipation, eyestrain, fatigue, and others, it seems more likely that poor posture is the result of such ailments and associated with them. In visual strain, for example, poor posture is the accommodation usually made to the inability to see well." Posture exercises given to the masses, without benefit of a differential diagnosis and without a prescription of exercise for each individual, are found to be somewhat of a waste or time.

Typical schoolroom or class posture drills are judged ineffectual, and it has now become understood that the following conditions must be met before much success in correcting bad posture by the application of exercise can be obtained:

— There must be a diagnosis made of the cause and nature of the postural variation before any exercise can be intelligently and scientifically applied.

— The exercise prescribed must be for the individual. Mass exercises indiscriminately applied are of little value. Each case is usually sufficiently different from others to require individual study and prescription.

— The exercises must be done faithfully, intensely, and over a prolonged period to have any effect. Experience in physical medicine points toward long exercise periods in which the subject works at the job diligently.

Postural deviations have many causes: congenital and genetic influences, nutritional deficiencies, disease and infection, faulty hearing and vision, muscular weakness, and psychological factors. In all these cases, regardless of cause, the condition usually results in some form of kyphosis, lordosis, or scoliosis, which in turn brings other changes in the general body configuration such as a forward head, uneven bips and shoulders, tipped pelvis, and sunken chest. The better programmes of physical education acknowledge the fact that there are postural deviations in individuals and conduct remedial or developmental posture work on the basis of the three conditions suggested above.

This is a very significant advance over the old scatter-gun technique of giving posture drills to all in the vain hope that all will profit. Such programmes are expensive in terms of time, teaching personnel, additional facilities, and medical consultation, but almost all administrators acknowledge their worth and will do all they can to insure their inclusion in the general curriculum. It should be emphasized that these posture programmes are not the same as the courses usually tagged "body mechanics," "basic activities," or "movement fundamentals."

The latter courses attempt to help the student discover himself through patterns of movement which require strength, agility, coordination, flexibility, and endurance and they may or may not include postural work. Obviously, physical education is committed to teaching the principles of general body alignment in the same way that mathematics is committed to teaching the multiplication tables and English to teaching the alphabet. It is also the responsibility of the intelligent physical educator to point out that very often a person moves and stands according to how he feels, and he certainly feels the way he carries himself. Attitudes can sometimes be changed through postural habits, as the teacher will emphasize by both teaching and example.

Whenever people are engaged in movement, there is always the possibility of injury. Injury to a young person is usually less disturbing, quicker to heal, and less frightening than the same injury to an older person. Children are fairly resilient when it comes to falls, and, not being mature enough to recognize the inherent danger in many activities, they are not beset with anxieties which hamper their performance. On the other hand, children are not usually as skilled as are the more mature and there is more chance for injury among the unskilled than there is with the skilled.

As a person grows older, he becomes more inhibited about his movement patterns. There is usually a point where an adult will actually refuse to do certain things if he believes that there is some possibility of injury. Sound physical education programmes will afford as little chance for injury as possible and will teach the student how to protect himself from injury later on. Not only must students be given the skills of activities; they must be taught how to use those skills safely and comfortably, and with maximum satisfaction. Although there is some question as to the physiological value of "warming up," the majority of physical educators still suggest its use. The idea, once held, that muscular viscosity was lowered during the warming-up process has not been supported by research. There is reason to believe that the internal temperature of the muscle is not really affected by warming up.

On the other hand, a good deal of research indicates that performance may be improved by participating beforehand in some exercise which is related to the task at hand, although whether improvement is due to neurological facilitation, better tonic response, or minute neuromuscular adjustments is not known. Research with subjects under hypnosis has suggested that the value of warm-up may be more psychological then psychological. At any rate, there appear to be more reasons to continue to utilize related warm-up drills than there are reasons to abandon them. If they help prevent injury, they should be used. The most common athletic injuries are sprains, strains, contusions, abrasions, and concussions.

Very often these injuries occur because of the position of the body when the blow was struck. It is essential to employ good mechanical principles in all movement patterns so that the risk of injury is lessened. Some sports call for productive equipment and it is up to the physical education teacher to see that it is worn. Shoulder pads will dissipate a blow in football and may be prevent a broken bone, shin guards will spread the blow of the hockey ball and prevent a contusion, a helmet may protect the head from brain injury in case of a direct hit by a baseball, and adequate strapping may avoid the risk of dislocation. Physical education teachers must convince participants that wearing protective equipment is not "sissy" but common sense.

Yet year after year there are more fatal accidents, on a percentage of participation basis, in this sport than any other. Even eliminating fatality, boxing still may cause irreparable damage. After a two-year study of boxers, concluded, "It is probable that no head blow is taken with impunity and that each knockout causes definite and irreparable damage." The danger is in the pinpoint hemorrhage or other brain injury. There are many portions of the brain in which destruction of a small amount of nerve tissue does not cause paralysis or other noticeable changes in behaviour. This is especially true in certain subcortical centers and of the cortex here the highest human faculties such as delicate coordination, memory, speech, self-control and the power of reasoning are lodged. Subsequent injuries add to earlier ones, since each is permanent. The exact location and the extent of each injury and the total of all injuries will determine the extent of loss of mental powers or bodily control.

A sound physical education programme will induce knowledge of first aid and effective care of the injured one an accident has occurred. At the times, medical advice should be sought in case of any serious injury or indeed in the case of any suspected injury. Overt symptoms are not always prospect and the wise physical educator will exercise prudence. Surely the personnel in physical education must accept the responsibility for the welfare of their charges, teaching no activity and organizing no experience which is likely to ignore the student's welfare.

The physical educator deals with exercise and with well-being. Traditionally, he had been thought of as something of an "expert" on keeping fit. His advice carries weight, not only with his students in school and college, but with a large segment of the public, who read what he writes and listen to what he says. And this is as it should be. The prospective teacher of physical education who has prepared himself well in his discipline and has gleaned from his studies the concept of the functioning of the totality that is man should know more than anyone else about man as he moves. In order to maintain his scientific and personal integrity, the physical educator must continually search for the truth and must forswear temptations to recommend unscientific and irrational theories, practices, and equipment. The country abounds with those who practice charlatanism under the guise of "physical culture," "physical training," "health salons," body development programmes, muscle building schemes, and weight reduction advice. Almost every city, town, and hamlet has it local "expert" who will offer to "make a man of the unfit," "shake pounds off the housewife," "reduce the hipline and add to the chest," and give life, strength, and joy" to anyone who will set foot in the establishment where he has set up headquarters.

8

Assessing Students Performance

Assessment plays an important part in the teaching-learning process at all levels of education. Since assessment plays such an important and significant part in the future of students there is no doubt that any assessment system will determine what students learn and the way in which they do this. Hence assessment will also determine the way in which we teach and what we teach.

But assessment is not just about grading and examinations. It is also about getting to know our students and the quality of their learning and to use this knowledge and understanding to their benefit. Assessment is without doubt one of the major 'drivers' of the teaching-learning process. It is thus important for teaching staff to be familiar not only with the technical aspects of the many different forms of assessment currently in use but also with their advantages and limitations and about assessment issues and concerns.

Assessment can take many forms, and it can be argued that the greater the diversity in the methods of assessment, the fairer assessment is to students. The art of assessing therefore needs to embrace several different kinds of activity. Whether we think of ourselves as lecturers, or teachers, or facilitators of learning, the most important thing we do for our students is to assess their work. It is in the final analysis the assessment we do that determines their diplomas, degrees, and future careers. Over the last decade, many of us have seen our assessment workload grow dramatically, as we work with increasing numbers of student, who are ever more diverse. Consequently, the time we have available to devote to assessing each student has fallen. It is therefore more important than ever to cultivate 'the art of assessing'.

Just as it seems to be assumed that anyone appointed to a teaching post in higher education can automatically teach, it is also implicit that they should be able to assess students' work. Many teachers in higher education wield their red pens for the first time without ever having had any real training in how to assess. Many are embarrassed at the notion of even asking for any guidance, yet are quite intimidated at the responsibility attached to assessing.

Teaching is a public affair, and we get all sorts of feedback regarding how well or how badly we teach - even without deliberately seeking feedback. The expressions on students' faces, the attendance at our classes, and the level of students' performance all help us to adjust our teaching techniques. Assessment, however, tends to be a private and intimate affair, and there is seldom anyone looking over our shoulders as we go about designing and implementing assessment. Given the importance of assessment, it is probably the aspect of our profession that should be scrutinised most carefully. Even with the best of intentions, external examiners and moderators can only contribute a limited amount to the processes of assessment, and the primary responsibility for assessment continues to rest with teachers.

One of the most useful benefits of assessment can be feedback gained by students on their performance regarding skills they are intended to develop, and their understanding of theories and concepts. It is an important part of the learning process for students to be able to learn from their mistakes as well as their triumphs. With larger class-sizes and increasing workloads, the time staff can devote to giving students detailed feedback on their work has been substantially eroded. It is therefore worth considering whether alternative forms of assessment (student peer-assessment in particular) can help increase the amounts of feedback which students can derive from assessed work.

There are many reasons for assessing students performance. Not all are good reasons. Some of the reasons are:

— we live in a society where people are appointed and employed on the basis of their qualifications.
— students themselves need feedback to help them to find out how their learning is going.
— we need feedback on how well students' learning is going, so that we can adjust and develop our teaching.
— assessment is often the major driving force which gets students down to serious studying.

Student assessment in physical education is based on self-assessment. The foundation of self-assessment rests on the social responsibility concept as it raises awareness within the student regarding his or her own behavior. The awareness of personal behavior is essential in situations that require teamwork and cooperation, but is also important for the students' personal success throughout life. Awareness is also crucial for future success, which provides an opportunity for the student to recognize possible mistakes and correct the mistakes by themselves. The student expectations provide guidelines for the students in regards to what is acceptable behavior and unacceptable behavior. This is why it is important that the students understand the student expectations provided to them during the first lesson. Students have easy access to the rules, as they are posted on the wall of the gymnasium where they have physical education. In the case of a situation where a student receives a middle or lower score the student must display an understanding of what he or she did wrong, which is the first step toward learning how to change the negative and maybe harmful behavior in regards to teamwork and self. Thus, self-assessment fosters personal responsibility that empowers the student and increases the students' self-efficacy.

Assessment is a comprehensive process that implies an assessment of the participants and the curriculum with which they interact. Assessment in physical education serves many purposes and contributes to decision making about: classification, diagnosis and guidance, motivation, reporting progress and program improvement.

Forms of Assessment

There are mainly three forms of assessment:

- *Student performance*: Students share in the assessment process. The needs of individual students are identified for the purpose of planning instruction; students are assessed for the purpose of selection and grouping; and parents/guardians are informed about students progress.
- *Teacher self-assessment*: Teachers self-appraise their efficacy in planning and 9 conducting lessons within the physical education, school and community contexts.
- *Curriculum improvement*: The suitability of instructional material and teaching methods are appraised to decide whether changes are needed.

Inherent in curriculum improvement is an ongoing assessment of the curriculum improvement criteria. Value orientations affect evaluative decisions. The Personal-Global orientation places equal emphasis on the learner, the facilitator, the activity, the knowledge base and the social context. Personal-Global evaluation guides students and teachers in learning how to deal critically and creatively with their educational settings, thus assisting in determining how to improve them. Teachers not only facilitate students' interaction during the physical education instructional periods, but also encourage the interaction to continue beyond the class setting. While broad social and environmental outcomes are stated, the process permits local\regional intentions to emerge.

Teaching-Learning-Evaluation Process

Student assessment is interconnected with outcomes, teaching methods and lesson planning. The Teaching-Learning-Evaluation Process implies that curriculum outcomes (intended or unintended), the selected teaching methods and student assessment are repeated throughout the teaching-learning-evaluation process. This Curriculum Framework recognizes diagnostic and formative assessment as being cumulative and guiding a summative assessment.

Assessing Student Performance

Assessing student performance is a process of collecting and interpreting information about the acquired knowledge, experiences, skills, attitudes and behaviour of learners as they interact in and with the curriculum. Operating within a Personal-Global orientation, assessment of progress is viewed as a cooperative and collaborative venture, done for and with learners as they make meaning of the curriculum. As students mature within a class and throughout the program, they take on more responsibility for their own assessment as part of the teacher's on-going assessment of student performance.

Learner outcomes about, in and through movement may be realized through activities that focus on learning processes, interlinked with self-actualization and social responsibility.

Learning Processes foster interactions, decision making, problem posing and problem solving. For example, in games at any level, students may work together in groups to discover and communicate a strategy to accomplish some specific goal. This could occur in a cooperative activity which requires a group to cross a spider's web; it could also work in a formalized game which requires a team to score a goal in scoop-ball or soccer. On a cognitive level the merit of a game or sport could be examined through dialogue with respect to it being cooperative while being competitive.

Self-Actualization fosters success and increased feelings of self-concept and self-esteem. For example, students may be guided to set personal goals through participation in a fitness unit, an outdoor adventure activity, or a formal game situation. Feelings of success or accomplishment may be expressed through group selection, or the drawing of happy and sad faces at the primary and elementary grades. At the intermediate and senior high levels, a series of questionnaires may be designed to assess student selfsatisfaction and feelings of accomplishment.

Social Responsibility fosters understanding and respect for others and the environment. Activities focus on becoming aware of inequity and injustice, and developing strategies for change. For example, students may reflect on formal games, pose problems and seek solutions related to inclusion and exclusion of classmates. Students may devise guidelines for the use and care of equipment, facilities and natural environmental settings, and set up ways to monitor the success of their action. For leadership projects, students may concentrate on their interests, and where and how they can make a positive contribution to their school and community.

Physical Education strives for the following general curriculum outcomes:

1. Perform efficient, creative and expressive movement patterns consistent with an active living lifestyle;
2. Demonstrate critical thinking and creative thinking skills in problem posing and problem solving relating to movement;
3. Assess attitudes and behaviours during activity in relation to self, the class, the school and the community;
4. Demonstrate socially responsive behaviour within the school and community; 10
5. Exhibit personal responsibility for the social, physical and natural environment during physical activity.
6. Exhibit personal development, such as positive self-esteem, self-responsibility, leadership, decision-making, cooperation, self-reflection and empowerment during physical activity;

Adjusting the Criteria for Student Assessment

Physical Education models, grounded in the Personal-Global orientation, place learners in an interactive role with the curriculum content and the environment. The Framework promotes a self-referenced and criterion-referenced approach founded on identifying educational intentions, and specific tasks that value and foster participation, involvement, responsibility and caring. Programs are student-teacher centered, in which flexible expectations with respect to activity skills and activity options are planned collaboratively by teacher and student.

Personal-Global assessment advocates:

— evaluation that assesses the process as well as the product;
— involvement with feedback for active participation, not just performance;
— self-management and self-assessment of attitude and behaviour toward physical activity and lifelong learning;
— self-reflection and collective-reflection about learning and the learning environment.

The Personal-Global curriculum orientation recognizes the merit of both qualitative and quantitative methods in the assessment of student progress. Assessment of personal meaning and social significance rely on qualitative methods. Teachers motivate learners to reflect on and record progress in interaction with others (cooperation, recognizing and resolving conflict), how specific lessons affect their attitudes, feelings, sense of self-esteem, and how specific activities affect their attitude and feelings about social and environmental conditions. Qualitative assessment methods allow new ideas and activities to emerge.

Assessment of student performance should rely on qualitative methods with quantitative methods supplementing or being used on occasion. Teachers may use qualitative and quantitative methods to assess the technical efficiency of the learner while performing the skill. In keeping with the collaborative nature as advocated by a Personal-Global orientation, teachers may have learners conduct technical assessments with their peers. Qualitative methods may also be conducted during formal and informal games where assessment would focus on who controls the play, or who gets possession rather than the score or final result.

Futuristic Strategy for Student Assessment

Participation and involvement with responsible decision making, behaviour and actions. Personal and social development serves as a starting point for developing a self-referenced and criterion-referenced approach to assessing participation and involvement. Teachers and students should explore assessment alternatives to supplement or replace traditional performance assessment.

Assessment based on participation and involvement will create opportunities for selfmanagement and self-assessment. Participation and involvement may be assessed throughout an activity unit, school year and/or grade level. Participation and involvement with responsible decision making, behaviour and actions provide a 'reference' for self-reflection and collective-reflection about personal development, and about issues of social and environmental significance in schoolcommunity settings. A self-referenced and criterion referenced approach that is studentteacher centered permits assessment to be conducted for and with learners as they interact in their physical education settings.

Assessment Instruments and Techniques

Contemporary assessment instruments may be adapted to implement a strategy for student assessment. Traditional performance tests become part of the process rather than being a summative result. Learners are taught how to use fitness and skill testing instruments, which they may select for self-assessment. To fully implement a humanistic strategy for student assessment, teachers and students must collaborate, experiment and reflect on new devices of assessment.

A sample of instruments that teachers and students may select from include:

— interest inventories that survey interest and/or awareness within specific activities or topics.;

— observation gathered and recorded through checklists, anecdotal records and rating scales;

— individualized task cards;

— individualized and group progress charts and files;

— self assessment based on informal and formalized journals, activity and exercise diaries/log books and activity records;

— peer assessment in which students are guided to collectively reflect on their experiences, achievements and weakness/deficiencies;

— teacher - student conferences based on structured and unstructured interviews;

— contracts based on the self-referenced criteria and negotiated between the student and teacher;

— discussions with reflection and time for follow up questionnaires;

— formalized fitness and skill testing if deemed appropriate or requested by an individual student, group or class;

— portfolios;

— teacher made tests based on appropriate criteria.

Reporting Progress

A Personal-Global orientation advocates qualitative

progress reporting to supplement the traditional quantitative (letter or numerical) reporting. Students become active participants in completing progress reports which must be flexible in adapting to age and ability groups. Reports need to be grade/level specific, but individualized to indicate progress in fitness, skill and movement, and include progress in practical projects and assignments where applicable. Specific to grade and/or levels, descriptive statements in the form of checklists or rating scales may be included to reflect participation, involvement, responsibility and caring, in balance with effort, improvement and achievement in skill and fitness.

Teacher Self-Assessment

The efficacy of teaching physical education may be considered as having two mutually intertwined components - (1) the outcomes to be achieved; and, (2) the extent to which the teacher creates a 'safe and friendly' educational environment consistent with the Personal-Global orientation. Teachers may personally assess their efficacy to empower students through two sets of qualities - critical/reflective qualities and technical qualities.

— *Critical/reflective qualities*: Teachers focus on the social context of their interactions with students and how these interactions are mediated in the day-today reality of the classroom, the gymnasium and other settings. Critical reflection relies on practical knowledge in the process of fostering empathy and empowerment of learners, and the promotion of change in society relative to physical education.

— *Technical qualities*: Teachers focus on their knowledge of content, their day-today behaviour during the instructional periods, and how this knowledge and behaviour affect student outcomes. It can also relate to coaching in schoolcommunity settings. The goal is to apply knowledge from pedagogy and sport science to improve the instructional process. The intent is to enhance physical activity, health and performance.

Teachers should cultivate their technical qualities to design and carry out efficient learning processes. They should also cultivate their critical/reflective qualities to examine the broader intentions of their instructional program and its relationship to society at large.

Self-Assessment of Critical/Reflective Qualities

There are three strategies for teachers to assess their critical/reflective qualities:

i) *Increase social knowledge* - In order to better respond to the needs and interests of students, teachers should continue to acquire knowledge about the nature of social life as it relates to physical education, and to complementary fields such as recreation and sport. Teachers are also encouraged to seek knowledge about the social construction of physical education knowledge.

ii) *Enhance academic/practical skills* - Teachers should continue to refine their literacy, numeracy, and communications skills and thinking to further their thinking or understanding about the social nature of physical education. Reflection emphasizes the application of principles in examining social issues in physical education. On becoming reflective, teachers learn to expose their thinking to others and open themselves to critique through dialogue and collaborative assessment.

iii) *Develop skills in critical discourse* - Teachers should examine their taken-forgranted practices and beliefs about physical education and strive for an open and continual process of revision. They go beyond the generic theories of teaching and learning to value their own personal theories of action which evolve from critically examined beliefs and past experiences.

Teachers of physical education, in collaboration with their peers, supervisors and students, may ask a series of critical/reflective questions about physical education programs and daily lessons:

1. Whose definitions of physical education, sport, play, and recreation are dominant and whose are discredited?
2. Which groups have traditionally benefited from the physical education class and the school program in general?
3. What are the relationships between physical education and other programs?
4. How can interactions during the physical education class make students aware of important moral and political questions such as equality and justice?

Self-Assessment of Technical Qualities

Teachers may use a series of questions based on the Teaching-Learning-Evaluation Process to self-assess their technical qualities:

— *Curriculum Planning* - Were the tasks planned progressively and developed in stages? Were lesson topics or activities sequenced appropriately?

— *Curriculum Content* - Did the learning tasks match the different levels of student ability? Were appropriate activities used?

— *Teaching and Learning Methods* - What teaching and learning strategies were applied? Did the strategies applied meet the differing needs of the learners? Were all learners provided with opportunities to progress?

The Personal-Global orientation encourages teachers to reflect on their self-assessment of technical qualities, and to become proactive in seeking a collaborative approach to teacher assessment.

Curriculum Improvement

To evaluate a physical education curriculum in any particular setting, the program must be viewed as having three basic components which are interrelated with program development - outcomes, activities and resources. Figure 1 shows this relationship, and provides a visual overview of curriculum development and evaluation.

Basic Components of Curriculum

Outcomes

Outcomes are the 'what' of the curriculum. They are the intentions or purposes that provide focus, direction and guidelines for the experiences that learners encounter as they interact in and with the curriculum. Chapter 3 outlines the broad intentions as general curriculum outcomes, which are further specified in more detailed key stage curriculum outcomes, more specific intents or expectations are outlined in Curriculum Guides.

Activities

Activities are the 'how' of the curriculum. They are what teachers and students are supposed to be doing in order to achieve curriculum outcomes. These activities or tasks include teaching and learning strategies.

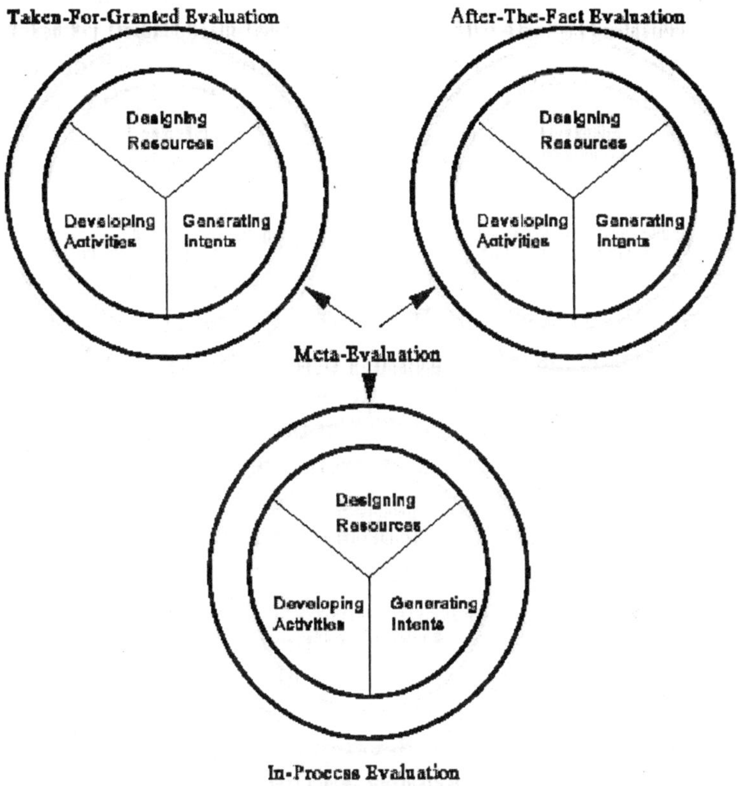

Figure 1. Visual overview of curriculum development

Resources

Resources are the 'with what' of the curriculum. They constitute resource persons, situations and equipment. Resource materials for specific grades and courses are authorized and recommended by the Department of Education.

Evaluation of Program Development

Taken-for-granted evaluation is the making of implicit values, beliefs and assumptions explicit during the process of development. The choice of intents, activities and resource materials involves a selection process among a choice of alternatives, some of which are deemed better or having greater worth. This selection, an ongoing activity during curriculum deliberations, is a form of evaluation, but is implicit and usually 'taken-forgranted'. The role of curriculum developers in this dimension is to become aware of the taken-for-granted nature of selection, to make explicit and to question the criteria used in selecting intents, activities and resources.

In-process evaluation is the explicitly planned 'formative' judging of the curriculum while it is being planned. It is imperative that opportunities be provided for continuous contact and exchange of ideas from the beginning, and throughout the process. Various kinds of formative procedures may be used, such as the validation procedures used in the development of this curriculum framework. A group of teacher/practitioners were selected to react to and suggest further direction for the refinement of this Framework. Other procedures could include workshops, where curriculum developers from various disciplines share developments in their field, and are exposed to other projects and professional literature.

Pilot-testing has been frequently used as a form of "in-process" evaluation of potential learning resources, where portions of a curriculum are tested in various settings. Generally, during the development of curriculum guides, specific activities and resources are piloted to determine suitability at grade levels or in various settings. Teachers are asked to keep daily journals of their concerns and recommendations on curriculum materials, or complete questionnaires which are then used by the development team to revise the curriculum. A more appropriate formative evaluation of the curriculum process calls for an involvement of the teacher/curriculum developer while engaged in teaching.

This form of curriculum development calls for an in-process evaluation in which individuals stand back and critically reflect upon their work. Critical questions posed by teacher/curriculum developers or a group of teachers and students invite clarification and further refinement of the curriculum process.

After-the-fact evaluation is that part of the development that occurs after the curriculum has been developed, piloted and implemented. This explicit 'summative' judging of the curriculum, while generally removed in time from the development phase, should be considered a continuation of the development process. In keeping with the view that evaluation is best undertaken as a cooperative and collaborative venture, the Framework advocates an "action research" approach to curriculum development and evaluation, where formative and summative evaluation merge into a series of reflective cycles. When curriculum development and evaluation is undertaken as action research, a cycle of collaborative renewal and reform may be possible in school and community settings.

Meta-evaluation is the evaluation of the evaluative design and method used for the inprocess and after-the-fact evaluation. It is an assessment of the formative and summative assessments of intents, activities and resources. Evaluation of evaluation keeps developers/ evaluators from being encapsulated within one specific orientation.

Exams

Traditional Exams

Traditional 'unseen' exams still make up the lion's share of assessment in education. Despite growing concern about the validity and fairness of this type of assessment, for all sorts of reasons it will continue to play a large part in the overall assessment picture.

Advantages

- Relatively economical. Exams can be more cost-effective than many of the alternatives (though this depends on economies of scale when large numbers of students are examined, and also on how much needs time and money needs to be spent to ensure appropriate moderation of students' performance).
- Equality of opportunity. Exams are demonstrably fair in that students have all the same tasks to do in the same way and within the same timescale.
- We know whose work it is. It is easier to be sure that the work being assessed was done by the candidates, and not by other people.

Disadvantages

- Students get little or no feedback about the detail of their performance, which is therefore wasted as far as feedback is concerned.
- Badly set exams encourage surface learning, with students consciously clearing their minds of one subject as they prepare for exams in the next subject.
- Technique is too important. Exams tend to measure how good students are at answering exam questions, rather than how well they have learned.

Tips on setting exam questions

- Don't do it on your own! Make sure you get feedback on each of your questions from colleagues. They can spot whether your question is at the right level more easily than the author. Having someone else look at one's draft exam questions is extremely useful. It is better still when all questions are discussed and moderated by teams of staff. Where possible, set questions with your colleagues. This allows the team to pick the best questions from a range of possibilities, rather than use every idea each member has.

— Ask colleagues: 'what would you say this question really means?'. If they tell you anything you hadn't thought of, you may need to adjust your wording a little.

— Keep your sentences short. You're less likely to write something that can be interpreted in more than one way if you write plain English in short sentences. This also helps reduce any discrimination to students whose second language is English.

— Work out what you're really testing. Is it decision-making, strategic planning, problem solving, data processing, or is it just too much dependent on memory? Most exam questions measure a number of things at the same time. Be up-front about all the things each question is likely to measure.

— Don't measure the same things again and again. For example, it is all too easy in essay-type exam questions to repeatedly measure students' skills at writing good introductions, firm conclusions, and well-structured arguments. Valuable as such skills are, we need to be measuring other important things too.

— Include data or information in questions to reduce the emphasis on memory. In some subjects, case-study information is a good way of doing this.

— Make the question layout easy to follow. A question with bullet points or separate parts can be much easier for (tense) candidates to interpret correctly than one which is just several lines of continuous prose.

— Don't overdo the standards. When you're close to a subject, it's easily possible that your questions get gradually harder year by year.

- Write out an answer to your own question. This will be handy when you come to mark answers, but also you'll sometimes find that it takes you an hour to answer a question for which candidates have only half-an-hour.
- Decide what the assessment criteria will be. Check that these criteria relate clearly to the syllabus objectives or the intended learning outcomes. Make it your business to ensure that students themselves are clear about these objectives or intended outcomes, and emphasise the links between these and assessment.
- Work out a tight marking scheme. Imagine that you are going to delegate the marking to a new colleague. Write it all down. You will find such schemes an invaluable aid to share with future classes of students, as well as colleagues actually co-marking with us, helping them to see how assessment works.
- Use the question to show how marks are to be allocated. For example, put numbers in brackets to show how many marks are attached to various parts of the question.
- Try your questions out. Use coursework and student assignments to give components of your future exam questions pilot runs, and use or adapt the ones that work best for exams.

Open-book Exams

In many ways these are similar to traditional exams, but with the major difference that students are allowed to take in with them sources of reference material. Sometimes, in addition the 'timed' element is relaxed or abandoned, allowing students to answer questions with the aid of their chosen materials, and at their own pace.

Advantages

These have many of the advantages of traditional exams, with the addition of:

— Less stress on memories! The emphasis is taken away from students being required to remember facts, figures, and other such information.

— Measuring retrieval skills. It is possible to set questions which measure how well students can use and apply information, and how well they can find their way round the contents of books and even databases.

— Slower writers helped? If coupled with a relaxation in the 'timed' dimension some of the pressure is taken away from those students who happen to be slower at writing down their answers.

Disadvantages

— Not enough books! It is hard to ensure that all students are equally equipped regarding the books they bring into the exam with them. Limited stocks of library books means that some students may be disadvantaged.

— Need bigger desks? Students necessarily require more desk-space for open-book exams if they are to be able to use several sources of reference as they compose their answers to exam questions. This means fewer students can be accommodated in a given exam room than with traditional unseen exams, and therefore open book exams are rather less cost-effective in terms of accommodation and invigilation.

Tips on setting open-book exam questions

All of the suggestions regarding traditional exam questions still apply. In addition

— Decide whether to prescribe the books students may employ. This is one way round the problem of availability of books. It may even be possible to arrange supplies of the required books to be available in the exam room.

— Set questions which require students to do things with the information available to them, rather than merely summarising it and giving it back.

— Focus the assessment criteria on what students have done with the information, and not just on them having located 'the correct information'.

— Expect shorter answers. Students doing open book exams will be spending quite a lot of their time searching for, and making sense of, information and data. They will therefore write less per hour than students who are answering traditional exam questions 'out of their heads'.

Structured Exams

These include multiple-choice exams, and several other types of formats where students are not required to write 'full' answers, but are involved in making true/false decisions, or identifying reasons to support assertions, or fill in blanks or complete statements, and so on. It is of course possible to design 'mixed' exams, combining free-response traditional questions with structured ones. In the following discussion, I will concentrate on the benefits and drawbacks of multiple choice questions, which also apply at least in part to other types of structured exam questions.

Advantages

— Greater syllabus coverage: it is possible, in a limited time, to test students' understanding of a much greater cross-section of a syllabus than could be done in the same time by getting students to write in detail about a few parts of the syllabus.

— Multiple choice exams test how fast students think, rather than how fast they write.

— Saving staff time and energy. With optical mark readers, it is possible to mark multiple choice exams very cost-effectively, and avoid the tedium and subjectivity which affect the marking of traditional exams.

— Testing higher-level skills? Multiple choice exams can move the emphasis away from memory, and towards the ability to interpret information and make good decisions.

Disadvantages

— The guess factor. Students can often gain marks simply by lucky guesses rather than correct decisions.

— Designing structured questions takes time and skill. It is harder to design good multiple-choice questions than it is to write traditional open-ended questions.

— Black and white or shades of grey? While it is straightforward enough to reward students with marks for 'correct' choices, it is more difficult to handle subjects where there is a 'best' option, and a 'next-best' one, and so on.

— The danger of impersonators? The fact that exams composed entirely of multiple-choice questions do not require students to give any evidence of their handwriting increases the risk of substitution of candidates.

Tips for designing multiple-choice exams

— Try out questions with colleagues and with large groups of students. Make sure that people are, on the whole, selecting correct options for the right reasons - and not because in one way or another the question gives away which is the correct option.

— Make sure that distractors are plausible. If no-one is selecting a given distractor, it is serving no useful purpose. Distractors need to represent anticipated errors in students' knowledge or understanding.

— Try to avoid overlap between questions. If one question helps students successfully to answer further questions, the possibility increases of students picking the right options for the wrong reasons.

— Pilot questions in formative-tests before using them in summative exams. Ideally, multiple-choice questions that appear in formal exams should be tried-and-tested ones. It is worth consulting the literature on multiple-choice question design and finding out how to assess the discrimination index and facility value of each question from statistical analysis of the performance of substantial groups of students.

— Write feedback responses to each option. Where possible, it is useful to be able to explain to students selecting the correct (or best) option exactly why their selection is right. It is even more useful to be able to explain to students selecting the wrong (or less-good) options exactly what may be wrong with their understanding. When multiple choice questions are computer-marked, it is a simple further step to get the computer to print out feedback responses to each student. This practice can equally be applied to formative multiple-choice tests, and to formal multiple-choice exams. Furthermore, the availability of feedback responses to each decision students make lends itself to extending the use of such questions in computer-based learning packages, and even computer-managed exams.

— Ensure that students are well-practised at handling multiple-choice questions. Answering such questions well is a skill in its own right, just as is writing open answers well. We need to ensure that students are sufficiently practised, so that multiple-choice exams measure their understanding and not just their technique.

— Look at a range of published multiple-choice questions. For example, several Open University courses have multiple-choice assignment questions, as well as multiple-choice exams. You may be surprised how sophisticated such questions can be, and may gain many ideas that you can build into your own question-design.

— Gradually build up a large bank of questions. This is best done by collaborating with colleagues, and pooling questions that are found to be working well. It then becomes possible to compose a multiple-choice exam by selecting from the bank of questions. If the bank becomes large enough, it can even be good practice to publish the whole collection, and allow students to practise with it.

Essays

In some subjects, assessment is dominated by essay-writing. Traditional exams often require students to write essays. Assessed coursework often takes the form of essays.

Advantages

— Essays allow for student individuality and expression. They are a medium in which the 'best' students can distinguish themselves.

— Essays can reflect the depth of student learning. Writing freely about a topic is a process which demonstrates understanding and grasp of the material involved.

— Students are used to writing essays. In many disciplines, essays represent the form of assessment which students are most familiar with. However, mature students often admit that the medium of assessment which worries them most is essays.

Disadvantages

— Essay-writing is very much an art in itself. Students from some backgrounds are disadvantaged regarding essay-writing skills as they have simply never been coached in how to write essays well. For example, a strong beginning, a coherent and logical middle, and a firm and decisive conclusion combine to make up the hallmarks of a good essay. The danger becomes that the presence of these hallmarks is measured time and time again, and students who happen to have perfected the art of delivering these hallmarks are repeatedly rewarded irrespective of any other strengths and weaknesses they may have.

— Essays take time to write. This means that assessment based on essay-writing necessarily is restricted regarding the amount of the syllabus that is covered directly. There may remain large untested tracts of syllabus.

— 'Write down the number we first thought of!' Essays are demonstrably the form of assessment where the dangers of subjective marking are greatest. Essay-marking exercises at workshops on assessment show marked differences between the mark or grade that different assessors award the same essay - even when equipped with clear sets of assessment criteria.

Tips on setting and using essay-type questions

Most of the suggestions given earlier in this article about writing traditional exam questions continue to apply - whether essays are to be used as assessed coursework or as exam questions. Some further suggestions are given below.

— Help students to see exactly how essays are marked. Alert students to the credit they gain from good structure and style. One of the best ways of doing this is to involve classes of students in looking at examples of past essays, and applying assessment criteria. This can be followed by involving students in peer-assessment of each others' essays.

— Help students develop the skills required to assemble the 'content' for essays. One of the best - and most time-effective - ways of doing this is to set class or coursework tasks which require students to prepare essay-plans rather than fully-finished masterpieces. A concept-map or diagram can show a great deal about the eventual 'worth' of students essays, and can avoid distraction from the elements of style and structure.

Practical Work

Many areas of study involve practical work, but it is often much more difficult to assess such work in its own right; assessing reports of practical work may only involve measuring the quality of the end-product of the practical work, and not the work itself.

Advantages

— Practical work may be really important. For example, none of us wants to be treated by a surgeon who has the best theoretical knowledge available, but whose practical work is slipshod!

— Employers may need to know how good students' practical work is. It is therefore useful to reserve part of our overall assessment for practical skills in such cases.

— Practical work is learning-by-doing. Increasing the significance of practical work by attaching assessment to it helps students approach such work more earnestly and critically.

Disadvantages

— It is often difficult to assess practical work in its own right. It is usually much easier to assess the end-point of practical work, rather than the processes and skills involved in their own right.

— It can be difficult to agree on assessment criteria for practical skills. There may be several ways of performing a task well, requiring a range of alternative assessment criteria.

— Students may be inhibited when someone is observing their performance. When doing laboratory work, for example, it can be very distracting to be watched!

Tips for assessing practical work

— Reserve some marks for the processes. Help students to see that practical work is not just reaching a defined end point, but is about the processes and skills involved in doing so successfully.

— Get students to self-assess how well they undertook tasks. This at least helps students to reflect on their performance in practical work, and since the overall contribution to their final grades of the process side of their work will probably be small, the risk of any error due to over-confidence or under-confidence is well worth the benefits accruing from reflection.

— Design the right end products. Sometimes it is possible to design final outcomes which can only be reached when the practical work itself is of high quality. For example, in chemistry, the skills demonstrated in the preparation and refinement of a compound can often be reflected in the purity and amount of the final product.

Portfolios

Building up portfolios of evidence of achievement is becoming much more common, following on from the use of Records of Achievement at school. Typically, portfolios are compilations of evidence of students' achievements, including major pieces of their work, feedback comments from tutors, and reflective analyses by the students themselves.

Advantages

— Portfolios tell much more about students. They can contain evidence reflecting a wide range of skills and attributes.

— Portfolios can reflect development. Most other forms of assessment are more like 'snapshots' of particular levels of development.

— Portfolios can relect attitudes and values as well as skills and knowledge. This makes them particularly useful to employers, looking for the 'right kind' of applicants for jobs.

Disadvantages

— Portfolios take a lot of looking at! It can take a long time to assess a set of portfolios. The same difficulty extends beyond assessment; even though portfolios may contain material of considerable interest and value to prospective employers, it it still much easier to draw up interview shortlists on the basis of paper qualifications and grades.

— Portfolios are much harder to mark objectively. Because of the individual nature of portfolios, it is harder to decide on a set of assessment criteria which will be equally valid across a diverse set of portfolios.

— The ownership of the evidence can sometimes be in doubt. It may be necessary to couple the assessment of portfolios with some kind or oral assessment or interview to authenticate the origin of the contents of portfolios, particularly when much of the evidence is genuinely based on the outcomes of collaborative work.

Tips on using and assessing portfolios

— Specify or negotiate intended learning outcomes clearly. Ensure that students have a shared understanding of the level expected of their work.

— Propose a general format for the portfolio. This helps students demonstrate their achievement of the learning outcomes in ways which are more easily assembled.

— Specify or negotiate the nature of the evidence which students should collect. This makes it easier to assess portfolios fairly, as well as more straightforward for students.

— Specify or negotiate the range and extent of the evidence expected from students. This helps students plan the balance of their work effectively, and helps them avoid spending too much time on one part of their portfolio while missing out important details on other parts.

— Don't underestimate the time it takes to assess portfolios. Also don't underestimate their weight and volume if you have a set of them to carry around with you!

— Prepare a pro-forma to help you assess portfolios. It is helpful to be able to tick off the achievement of each learning outcome, and make decisions about the quality of the evidence as you work through a portfolio.
— Use post-its to identify parts of the portfolio you may want to return to. This can save a lot of looking backwards and forwards through a portfolio in search of something you know you've seen in it somewhere!
— Consider using post-its to draft your feedback comments. You can then compose elements of your feedback as you work through the portfolio, instead of having to try to carry it all forward in your mind till you've completed looking at the portfolio.
— Provide interim assessment opportunities. Give candidates the opportunity to receive advice on whether the evidence they are assembling is appropriate.

Presentations

Giving presentations to an audience requires substantially different skills from writing answers to exam questions. Also, it can be argued that the communications skills involved in giving good presentations are much more relevant to professional competences needed in the world of work. It is therefore increasingly common to have assessed presentations as part of students' overall assessment diet.

Advantages

— There is no doubt whose performance is being assessed. When students give individual presentations, the credit they earn can be duly given to them with confidence.

— Students take presentations quite seriously. The fact that they are preparing for a public performance usually ensures that their research and preparation are addressed well, and therefore they are likely to engage in deep learning about the topic concerned.

— Presentations can also be done as collaborative work. When it is less important to award students individual credit for presentations, the benefits of students working together as teams, preparing and giving presentations, can be realised.

Disadvantages

— With large classes, a round of presentations takes a long time. This can be countered by splitting the large class into groups of (say) 20 students, and facilitating peer-assessment of the presentations within each group on the basis of a set of assessment criteria agreed and weighted by the whole class.

— Some students find giving presentations very traumatic! However, it can be argued that the same is true of most forms of assessment, not least traditional exams.

— The evidence is transient. Should an appeal be made, unless the presentations have all been recorded, there may be limited evidence available to reconsider the merit of a particular presentation.

— Presentations can not be anonymous. It can prove difficult to eliminate subjective bias.

Tips on using assessed presentations

— Be clear about the purposes of student presentations. For example the main purpose could be to develop students' skills at giving presentations, or it could be to cause them to do research and reading and improve their subject knowledge. Usually, several such factors may be involved together.

— Get the students to establish a set of assessment criteria for their own presentations. You may be pleasantly surprised how good their criteria are. When students have a sense of ownership of the criteria, they tend to work much harder to achieve them.

— Ensure that the assessment criteria span presentation processes and the content of the presentations sensibly. It can be worth reserving some marks for students' abilities to handle questions after their presentations.

— Consider using student peer-assessment of their presentations. Make up grids using the criteria which have been agreed, allocating each a weighting, and get all of the group to fill in the grids for each presentation. The average peer-assessment mark is likely to be at least as good an estimate of the relative worth of each presentation as would be the view of a single tutor doing the assessment.

— Consider giving students some prior practice at assessing presentations. It is useful, for example, to give students a dry run at applying the assessment criteria they have devised, on one or two presentations on video. The discussion which this produces usually helps to clarify or improve the assessment criteria.

Vivas

Viva-voce exams have long been used to add to or consolidate the results of other forms of assessment. They normally take the form of interviews or oral examinations, where students are interrogated about selected parts of work they have had assessed in other ways.

Advantages

— Vivas are useful checks on the ownership of evidence. It is relatively easy to use a viva to ensure that students are familiar with things that other forms of assessment seem to indicate they have learned well.

— Vivas seem useful when searching for particular things. For example, vivas have long been used to help make decisions about borderline cases in degree classifications.

— Candidates may be examined fairly. With a well-constructed agenda for a viva, a series of candidates may be asked the same questions, and their responses compared and evaluated.

Disadvantages

— Some candidates never show themselves well in vivas. Cultural and individual differences can result in some candidates underperforming when asked questions by experts and figures of authority.

— The agenda may 'leak'. When the same series of questions is being posed to a succession of students, it is quite difficult to ensure that candidates who have already been examined aren't able to commune with friends whose turn is still to come.

— The actual agenda covered by a viva is usually narrow. Vivas are seldom good as measures of how well students have learned and understood large parts of the syllabus.

Tips on using vivas

— Prepare the agenda in advance, and with colleagues.

It is dangerously easy for the agenda to develop during a series of interviews with different students.

— Prepare and use a checklist of pro-forma to keep records. Memory is not sufficient.

— Ensure there are no surprises. Share the agenda with each candidate, and clarify the processes to be used.

— Work with one or more colleague. Divide the agenda of questions, so that there can be an observer at each point as well as a questioner.

— Try to put students at ease at the beginning. For example, ask something very straightforward, or simply chat for a moment or two about something quite irrelevant to the viva.

— De-brief each viva at once. Even if only for a minute or two, it pays to discuss briefly impressions and findings after each interview, and to make brief notes of conclusions.

Innovative Assessment

Innovative assessment could be any form of assessment which involves the application of a new technique or method. For us, however innovative assessment has come to mean more than that. It is a term we use which encompasses a whole range of different techniques and methods, not all of which are new inventions. What unites them is a common goal: to improve the quality of student learning. Innovative assessment is also about what Heron called 'the redistribution of educational power' when assessment becomes not just something which is 'done to' learners but also 'done with' and 'done by' learners. Assessment should be primarily for the learners and for learning.

All too often, assessment is associated with the end-product of the learning process oath emphasis given to measurement, evaluation, grading and social acceptance. But there is more to the process of assessment than establishing whether or not you can attend the 'passing-out parade' or whether your name will be read out first or last at the graduation ceremony. As the table below demonstrates assessment can be used to perform a number of different functions: it can be used as both carrot and stick.

According to Harris and Bell assessment is also carried out for three different groups of people: the learners, the teachers, and the 'outsiders'. It could be argued that traditional methods of assessment, although perhaps not intentionally, have sometimes tended to overlook the needs of the learner in an attempt to provide readily accessible and comparable results for others e.g. teachers, employers, parents, and government statisticians. The output from many forms of innovative assessment (e.g. profiles, portfolios, pro-formas) however, lend themselves much less readily to quantification and the production of league tables of 'performance'.

The learner is the only group for whom all the different functions of assessment are performed, in reality this isn't always the case. In some cases assessment by-passes the needs of the learner. For example, in any form of assessment it is usually beneficial for the learner to receive detailed feedback indicating their strengths and weaknesses in the area of assessed work and suggesting areas where improvements or changes might be made in the future. If however. learners only receive a single, all encompassing mark or grade for a piece of assessed work, however good or bad that mark may be, the learner is unaware of precisely what aspects of the work were strong or weak. Consequently, the assessment fails to perform any formative (feedback giving) function in the learning process. One can see how ridiculous this situation would be in a vocational subject, such as medicine: imagine if during your training at university you got six out of ten for performing a heart triple by-pass operation on a dummy but were never told what you lost the four marks for! Fortunately, this situation is unlikely to occur with a vocational course, such as medicine, as assessment in such subjects is predominantly 'criterion referenced': to pass the student has to demonstrate that they are 'competent' in certain skills.

Although it is obviously problematic, primarily because it is a danger to the public, to let a medical student graduate without telling them what they are doing right or wrong, it is quite common for a student to graduate in less vocational subjects, such its sociology and geography, knowing only that they performed better than X and worse than Y but not really knowing where, if anywhere, they went wrong and how they could improve on their performance in the future. The learner is left fumbling in the dark without a guide. Often it is simply a lack of communication that prevents assessment from serving the needs of the learner, the teacher is aware of their strengths and weaknesses but these are not communicated effectively to the learner, without this knowledge the learner is powerless. Innovative assessment, in contrast, is about finding ways to empower the learner.

So what are the aims of innovative assessment? Some might even say: "what's the point in changing an assessment system that has served us so well for so many years?" But has the system really 'served us well'? Much of the impetus for innovation and change in the assessment process stems from a general dissatisfaction with traditional methods of assessment and a shared belief that these methods rather than enhancing and facilitating the learning process actually stifle deep learning and creative thinking. Many innovators would therefore challenge the belief that the existing system served us well. Innovative assessment is not just some trendy, new technique dreamt-up purely to save on the amount of time teachers spend on marking, it is a genuine attempt to improve the quality of learning in higher education. If we do save time in the process then all the better for our own learning.

In the context of student assessment therefore, innovation aims to achieve several specific outcomes.

Firstly, it aims to produce students who are:

— 'deep' rather than 'surface' learners
— highly motivated and committed
— enterprising
— equipped with a range of transferable skills
— capable of self-criticism and evaluation
— fairly and reliably assessed
— active and reactive participants in the learning process, capable of 'creative dissent' rather than simply passive, uncritical recipients of other people's knowledge.

Secondly, it aims to produce a more fertile learning environment and a more rewarding learning experience for all teachers and students.

Another guide to be published later in this series, Assessment: an innovators guide, provides an introduction to some of the techniques and methods more commonly employed by innovators' in an attempt to achieve some of these aims and offers some practical tips on how to reduce the risks of failure.

Before one can start to implement changes in the way students are assessed one has to deal with the skeptics, those who will resist change of any kind, and those who tried it once, found it didn't work and so dropped it altogether. Some teaching staff delight in telling others horror stories about so and so's 'famous failure' with innovative assessment, usually concluding the story with those well worn words of warning: 'Is that what you want? Cause that's what'll happen.' While we would be the first to concede that innovative assessment practices are not without their problems and do require careful and considered application if they are to be successful, there is much misinformation bandied about to prevent one from even considering the possible benefits which might be attained from changing the present assessment system. Many people still regard innovative assessment practices with a great deal of suspicion and have several misgivings about their supposed benefits. The lists presented on the following pages, therefore, are an attempt to allay some of the fears and to answer some of the more common criticisms of innovative assessment practices. They are a compilation of our own remaining nagging doubts about innovative assessment together with the concerns more commonly expressed to us by other members of staff.

9

Evaluation of Physical Education Programmes

By their very nature physical education and school health education have many things in common. They frequently are taught by the same personnel and administered by the same person. In fact many persons both in and out of education are unable to distinguish between them. Actually, there is enough difference to warrant their recognition as two aspects of a total educational programme. They share a common goal—the development of health—but physical education is concerned also with the cultivation of leisure-time skills and the social orientation of people so necessary in preserving the techniques of living in the democratic way. Only if the latter two are thought of a related to a very broad concept of health can the whole aim of physical educational be thought of as health building. In materials and technique they are, of course, more different than alike.

Physical education uses as its mediums the movements of dance, games, and sports. It educates through doing, through motor expression. Health education implies the acquisition of knowledge about health and the participation in healthful practices, leading into a life lived in full reflection of the science of healthful living. Both are educational enterprises, both are productive of improved behaviour and richer living, yet their ways of arriving at their ends, the tools they use, are different. Physical education, for example, is often mistaken for a health programme. It is thought of an entirely health-building, and if health is not built then something is wrong. A good programme of physical education will, of course, not detract from the health of its participants, but there are also other ends it must meet and it cannot be expected to have as much influence on health as some persons believe.

When the two programmes, physical education and health education, can meet on common ground and prosper together, the students benefit. In such instances, the programme of activities, which is certainly desirable from the standpoint of growth and development, it flanked by programmes of health appraisal, disease control, mental health, instruction, emergency care, and nutritional services. Then the circle is complete and school health education and physical education are seen as complementary areas.

Nothing can be tolerated in physical education which detracts from the health of students, and every detail of the programme should be an example of the best of healthful practice. Programmes of physical education contribute to organic strength and development and to personal resources of a psychological nature. Administrators, however, must go farther. They must present an environment which is faultless from the standpoint of health and a programme of care which is perfect in its operation.

From the early days of organized physical education down to the present, there has existed a fine and close relationship between physicians and physical educators. Many of the early college programmes were administered by physicians, and today a large school or college programme usually has a medical adviser on its staff. The success of school programmes is dependent in many respects upon medical advice. There are three principal points of contact between the physical education programme and the medical adviser to the school: in the classification process, in councelling on health problems of students.

ADMINISTRATION

A physical education programme is made up of a limited number of activities; although it possesses facilities for more, no additions are ever made because of some small administrative obstacle which seems insurmountable at the time. One sees programmes of vigorous physical education without towels for bathing, without lines on the field, with makeshift bases on the diamonds, with sleepy and unambitious teachers, and with locker rooms which would profit from the use of a broom. such matters are administrative. They are marks of inefficiency or ineptness which jeopardize the value of the physical education programmes in the eyes of the student. It is not intended to convey the impression that all administration has been faulty. That would be far from the truth. Hundreds of high schools and colleges have effective, useful, and skillfully handled programmes. In them administrative practices have evolved in full consciousness of the needs of children, the relative case with which these needs can be met, and the determination to make of physical education a force for democratic living. It is this concept of administration which not only is mirrored in effective programmes but has the humility to understand that, rather than being an end in itself, administration is merely the means by which educational good can come to young people.

The good administrator sees himself as a sort of executive servant, one who carries out the will, meets the needs, executes the desires of the group. He is responsive to group action, he participates in the formation of group opinion, he seeks and distributes information on the problems, at hand, he guides group thinking into orderly channels; but in the end he administers the programme in terms of the expressed wisdom of the group. He merges his own ideas with those of his colleagues as they seek the best solution to the problems at hand. Such an administrator conceives of his job as that of making others comfortable, of facilitating teaching, of enhancing the richness of the programme.

True democratic administration seeks to serve, not dominate; guide, not order; and act, not defer. As has been said, physical education, unlike some other curriculum areas, calls for a large amount of administration. Planning, purchasing, organizing, and evaluating are companion functions to teaching. Modern teaching methods must be accompanied by modern administrative practice. Democratic methods in the classroom must be met by similar methods elsewhere. Teaching, always the heart of any programme, is placed in bad light if the other functions are not well coordinated with it. To construct an adequate programme for all the students in any given school requires, therefore, that thought be given to the character of democratic administration as it faces the following key problems.

It has been said that the structure of the school system in the United States is determined in large measure by the ideal of equality of opportunity through education. An observer might believe that the physical education programmes of the schools and colleges come as close as any to meeting this ideal. Gymnasiums swarm with players, outdoor playgrounds are crowded, and roaring crowds cheer their favourites. The benefits of physical education appear to have been spread well over the school population.

A modern complete programme contains adapted activities for the handicapped, intramural sports for those somewhat less skilled than varsity players, widely popular varsity contests, class instruction for all, and free-play opportunities. The framework is there: the potentialities are real. The crowds could be accommodated. Actually, however, equal opportunities for a physical education are not extended to all alike or even to all in relation to their abilities. There are millions of children in thousands of schools who have no physical education instruction of any kind. And there are thousands of systems where inequalities of opportunity as between boys and girls, the skilled and the unskilled, the older and the younger children, are so striking as to lead one to believe, that we have just begun to extend the privileges of physical education democratically to all students.

The intelligent administrator harbours the ambition to give every student his chance, to provide facilities, time, and personnel to all groups; he does not remain complacement in the face of obvious inequalities. For example there are generally gross inequalities between programmes provided for girls and those for boys. Because boys are expected to be more skilled at sports than girls, the unthinking public, accepts, in fact demands, that boys be given the best field houses, the best pools, more space, more teachers, than girls are given. If a new gymnasium is to be built, the girls will inherit the old one. If the only floor is in demand after school, the boys are likely to get it. If limited financial resources are to be divided, the boys will draw the lion's share. Administration of that sort makes a mockery out of efforts to teach democracy through physical education. The ideal of equality is attained in some schools, where fine, well-balanced programmes exist. Some colleges also have extended appropriate opportunities to all students.

But there are still school systems, cities, counties, and states where opportunity in physical education needs to be reviewed to locate the inequalities and provide appropriate budgets, facilities, and personnel to rectify them. It should be well understood that a free and universal access to education, in terms of the interest, ability and need of the student, must be a major goal of American education.

The time has come to make physical education and make recreation equally accessible to all, without regard for race, creed, sex, or national origin. Where boys and girls of all origins are attending the same school, physical education must put an end to its discriminating favouritism and develop a complete programme in which instruction and play opportunities are extended freely to everyone. Responsibility for the attainment of equal opportunities belongs to the administrator of the programme. What we mean realistically is that, if priorities must be established for the general development of a complete programme, the basic instruction programme for all boys and girls should be placed first. This principle is valid at all levels of education from elementary school through college.

Equality Among Students

This phase of a complete programme finds its origin in the wholly democratic notion that the best is entitled to a full opportunity to develop his skill just as is the poorest. Democracy in education has never meant the glorification of mediocrity. The superior have rights equal to those of the inferior. As we translate this into physical education, we conceive of the competitive programmes between school teams as mediums by which the best can enjoy their rightful development and be tested against their equals.

There are excellent reasons for considering the competitive athletic programme an integral part of the curriculum of any school or college. The educational opportunities within athletics are real and worth while. They are, however, lost in some places through inept administration, and in others the programme is administered so undemocratically that the potential values become submerged under an avalanche of monopoly, favouristism, and special privilege. The abuses of the democratic ideal in athletics have seriously hurt the programme, distortions in budgets, exorbitant salaries paid to coaches of teams, gifts for players, inequalities in facilities and equipment, all throw a cloud over what might be the finest glory of a democratically administered programme. What would characterize the democratic administration of competitive athletics? These might be some of the earmarks:

— There would be no distinction between major and minor sports. All rewards would be of the same value and size. All sports are major to the participant, and his interests are all that count in athletics.

— No interscholastic sport would be organized until the general programme for the majority was well established. In some schools a basketball team is organized first. This is putting the cart before the horse. The majority should be served-and then the skillful minority.

— Once the extensive and intensive programmes were both established, they would grow together, improving and enriching as time passed and neither drawing the life blood of facilities, personnel, or finance away from the other.

— Scholastic-eligibility rules as prerequisites to sport participation would disappear, and all would be welcome to try out regardless of individual academic background or financial status. The student would be a bona-fide student of the school, in good standing, and subject to all of its rules and regulations, or not play.

— Athletics would be conducted and administered by thoughtful, professionally prepared people, not by the miscellaneous, run of expedintly chosen popular figures. Athletic boards, faculty managers, conference representatives would become wholly advisory and useful in keeping the programme institutional and not the plaything of vested interests.

— Policy, practice, and procedures would be arrived at by discussion and not by fiat. When college athletics, for example, find it necessary to employ a national "czar" to make and enforce rules, the administration of athletics locally has forfeited an important prerogative of democratic education.

— Coaches would not be employed and disposed of in terms of their colourful personalities, or the score on the scoreboard.

— The athletic programmes, both interscholastic and intramural, would be regulated as a part of an all-school "activities council," whose membership would include representatives from the students and from music, dramatics, art, administration, and other activity interests. Such a council would coordinate all activities allowing none to monopolize or dominate the programme at the expense of others.

Currently there are well-developed programmes of sports "within the walls" in thousands of schools and colleges. When well conceived and administered, they provide competitive experience to many students who otherwise would not have it. Just as in other aspects of the total programme, thoughtless administrative policy can seriously impair the good which is inherent in intramural programmes. To keep intramural sports wholly within their original and democratic perspective, these characteristics could well be preserved;

1. The programme should serve all students by providing participation outlets no manner how small the group.
2. The programme can well grow out of the basic instructional programme and provide an opportunity for the practice of the activities learned in class.
3. The programme should exclude no one, honour all who are deserving, be arranged to retain as many teams and individuals for the whole season as possible, and show no faouritism whatsoever as regards class, race, or any other distinction.
4. Intramural programmes sometimes are allowed to succumb for the lure of the champion. The desire to attain supremacy, to recognize a champion, may cause the administration to use elimination rather than round-robin tournaments, and to neglect sports such as folk dancing or skating in favour of basketball and softball where championships will not be the guiding motive in democratically administered programmes.
5. Nor will awards be the principal outcome. Originally, intramural players played for the true and abiding values within the games-for fun, for friendship, or for the exhilaration which comes from testing one's skill against that of one's contemporaries. Such simple pleasures were naturally supplemented by prestige and social approval. Those rewards, inherent in the game situation, were no allowed to remain long as the natural lures for participants.

6. Intramural programmes provide fine opportunities for the development and exercise of student leadership. Teams can be coached, managed, and captained by students; student committees can have a part in policy and administration. Officiating can be done by students. The chance is therefore a fine type of democratic experience. It is unfortunate when intramural sports fall into the hands of promoters who "ballyhoo" for 100 per cent attendance or who honour champions with rewards out of proportion to achievement. Or when the games become not so much friendly contests as brawls between clubs or classes who seem willing to resort to any verbal or fistic excess in order to win a game.
7. The intramural facilities should be of the best. All players are equal in their title to facilities, space, and equipment. Thus, the intramural player need not inherit the ball worn out by the varsity. Both should have new balls. The intramural softball diamond should be as well as groomed as the varsity diamond, and officials should be as competent. Like standards applied to these twin programmes would do much to convey a feeling of equality of opportunity to the rank and file of student.

It is a great mistake to believe that modern physical education is only for the strong or the athletic. No such distinction is tenable. If a youngster is well enough to be in school he is well enough to receive a physical education adapted to his need and condition. The responsibility belongs to the administration and the teacher to find and teach activities suitable to each child and to construct a programme flexible enough to allow for adaptations to individual needs and limitations. The psychologically maladjusted, the timid, the obese, the cardiac, the crippled, the blind, the injured-all of these exceptional cases and many others are entitled to the pleasures which come from learning through physical education, from achieving skill in some active recreation, and from group participation. Democratically speaking, they are obviously as entitled as anyone else to a physical education geared to their possibilities.

Two courses of action commonly have been pursued with handicapped pupils. The first has been to excuse the child and the second has been to place him in a "corrective programme." Neither course of action has been found adequate in terms of the child's total needs or the potentialities of the school for meeting these needs. Excusing the child from physical education has been regarded as a safe way out, but it is costly to the child. It is true, that it may keep him from aggravating his condition or from incuring new injury. Also it prevents embarrassment and frustration in a programme generally recognized as being beyond his capabilities. In instances where the school offers only a general programme of physical education there is considerable justification for excusing the pupil. But excusing him is not meeting his needs. He is a human being in a free society seeking to live and grow with others of his age group despite the fact that he must live within the limitations imposed by his disability. In so far as possible he wants to be like others. He is seeking help from his school and he feels badly let down when an oversimplified solution to his problem, such as excusing him from activity, is resorted to by those from whom he is seeking help. The study hall is a poor alternative to engaging in selected activities with other in his own social group.

The second great war taught many the importance of physical education to the injured. Following the war some colleges made the unwarranted decision to exclude or excuse all veterans from the physical education programme. This immediately not only denied the veteran who was physically uneducated a chance to learn his tennis, or golf or swimming but also excluded from the programme thousands of men who were casualties and who would have profited organically, psychologically, or both from a controlled physical education experience. In colleges where the casualty was given more sympathetic treatment blinded men learned to swim, amputees to play golf; injured muscles and joints were reeducated; and many an unsocial point of view or a feeling of futility was dispersed by the experience of working profitably in a planned programme of physical education.Such programmes can rightfully begin in the elementary years and extend through school and college. Individuals in need of special attention. special gear, special instruction, individuals who need restricted rather than unlimited activity, can be found and dealt with profitably by competent teachers, administrators, and physicians working together. Children as well as adults can benefit from this kind of individualized physical education. This form of physical education, variously called individual physical education, adapted physical education, corrective physical education is defined as a "diversified programme of developmental activities, games, and sports, suited to the interests, capacities and limitations of those who may not safely or successfully engage in unrestricted participation in the vigorous activities of the general programme. The need for such adaptations is clear not only in terms of the numbers of children who would profit but in terms of value which can accrue to each child from a well administered programme.

Grouping of Studnets

Physical education being a required element in the curriculum teachers have experienced overloaded classes, heavy schedules, and heterogeneous groups. In some places physical education has been the dumping ground for all students who were not otherwise occupied at any particular hour. It was natively assumed that since any number could be exercised at the same time what matter if a class contained over a hundred students ranging from seventh to twelth graders? Under such punishing conditions volleyball can be played with twenty-four on a side! Or a single line is formed and the leader runs the class in a childish configuration on the gymnasium floor. In a circumstances like these, physical education had better be abandoned. A little is worse than none at all because of the boredom, frustration, and sense of futility created.

Modern physical education attempts to classify its students in order to approximate homogeneity in its groupings. This is done by means of screens and tests of various kinds. The first screen, of fundamental importance, is the physical or medical examination. This is vital to physical education; it tells what members are able to participate in the normal vigorous. programme and which ones should seek adapted activities. After such an examination two groups appear in place of one. Depending upon the care with which the examination is given, and the standards used for placement in the adapted groups, there till usually be from 2 to 15 per cent of secondary school and college students in the adapted programme. The rest will be available for the regular instruction of the classes.

Skill, fitness, strength, experience are some which can be measured; students with similar scores can be put together in squads or sections or hours. For example, those who hold fitness and strength to be the principal outcomes of physical education find a strength of fitness test-of which there are several-useful in separating the weak from the strong. The weak may be given strength-building exercises. No use in giving them to the strong; they are already strong! Likewise, for those who see physical education as an experience in the acquisition of recreational skills, there would be no use teaching a high school girl to swim if she already knew how-or to folk dance, or play tennis, if she were already skilled in these. So tests of skill, knowledge, and appreciation have been developed.

When administered they inform the teacher where the elementary students are, the intermediate, and the advanced; where the dub is and who is the expert. By such means teaching can be geared to needs and placed where it will do the most good. In some programmes it has been possible to excuse some students from class attendance altogether because they already know or can perform up to the standard expected of them at the conclusion of the term's work. These superior students are given the opportunity to help teach others who are less skilled, to serve in some capacity in other aspects of the programme, to seek instruction in some activity with which they are unfamiliar, or, in some instances, to omit physical education entirely from their programme. Such testing of student ability and knowledge is quite in accord with evaluating procedures used elsewhere in the curriculum.

There are mathematics placement tests, english proficiency tests, spelling tests, and many others aimed at determining pupil status so as to gear instruction to needs. It is considered better practice to have smaller groups of students with similar needs than larger groups with a variety of needs. Thus the theory of homogeneous grouping can be applied to physical education advantageously. The teacher can do a better job of teaching if;

1. he knows the student as an individual,
2. the student is given some individual attention and instruction, and

3. there is just enough variety in the group to stimulate all of them to improve.

The tests, whether of fitness, ability, strength, knowledge, or appreciation, serve as screens following the physical examination. Some of them are better than others. They are certainly not interchangeable, because they evaluate different things. They should be used in relation to the aims of the programme. If the aim is to develop strength, then strength test should be used to screen out those who are already strong. If knowledge is the desired outcome, then knowledge test must be developed. If the programme aims for all-around recreational ability, or for the development of social understandings, screens for these must be used. For students who are screened out early by the physical examination, there should follow immediately a more thorough screen consisting of a follow-up examination and personal conference between physician and teacher. At this conference the kind of physical education appropriate to the individual student can be arranged. Here is the ultimate in the individualized programme. The former practice of giving mass therapeutic or corrective exercises is no longer in good repute. If a few students with problems sufficiently alike can be taught successfully in groups, such groups are arranged; but the modern programme no longer assembles all "posture cases" for a half-hour of indiscriminate "posture work," nor are posture exercises applied indiscriminately to a class of fifty or a hundred children without knowing who needs them. To administer a programme in the democratic pattern, then, means to move away from impersonal mass activities at any level and to seek closer teacher pupil relationships as a means of discovering and answering individual needs.

Many programmes allow students to elect their activities within the schedule for the semester or year. Such an arrangement is possible only when facilities and supervision can be provided two or more groups at the same time. If for example, a school has more than one indoor exercise room, available outdoor facilities, and perhaps a pool, it should be possible for one eleventh-grade group to elect swimming, another basketball, another tumbling. There would have to be adult or competent squad leader supervision to oversee the various groups, because student groups should not be actively engaged without some responsible person in change. Elections are made either as a result of proficiency tests or merely as free choice. Occasionally a high school or college programme administers a proficiency test as described in preceding paragraphs. Successful scoring on the test brings certain privileges and one of them could be to choose any activity offered that semester. Other programmes, particularly at the college level, offer several different sports each hour and student may choose the one to their liking. On any such elective plan it is important to have some guidance. There would be little point to electing a sport in which the student is already proficient.

Physical education is not merely a play period. It is supposed to bring students greater abilities, deeper understandings, than they had when they enrolled. Progress must be shown. Hence, if a student elects to do something he already can do well, be is in no position to profit very much from his experience. He needs guidance in selecting some other activity which will be new to him or in which he can make some progress. Without guidance a high school letter winner in basketball can elect more basketball all four semesters of his college requirement and thus widen his experience with physical education activities little if at all students should constantly be advised to try new things. It is like reading new books-one seldom spends the whole semester reading the same book over again. The gain one gets from basketball after six or seven years of it gets pretty meagre. It becomes more of a pastime and less of an instrument for education.

The participation of students not only in curriculum planning but in the actual conduct and administration of the class and programme is important to their understanding of democracy. in action. Specifically, every reasonable opportunity should be taken to allow them to share in planning, teaching, and administration. They cannot be expected to understand the democratic process if they never witness it or participate in it. Committees should help plan the semester's programme, arrange the squads, secure the equipment. Students can arrange tournaments, explore new activities, inventory facilities. They can give tests, teach others less skilled, and in many ways share in the organization of the physical education experiences. Physical education programmes make little contribution to the preservation of democracy if they are conducted by and through authoritarianism.

Teaching Standards

The physical education teacher may have either or both of two opportunities in regard to health instruction. He may be asked to organize and conduct the specific teaching of health in the curriculum. If so, the class should be organized separately from physical education. It will be less effective if it shares, say, one hour a week with the activity programme. If health is to be taught, it should be given status and not thought of as an appendage to physical education or anything else. The second opportunity is to correlate the instruction given in physical education with the broad area of personal and community health. The physical education teacher is surrounded by opportunities to teach health, and a student could not attend a single physical education class without having some experience bearing upon his health.

The important thing for the teacher to secure is the best in correlation and experience.

The personal standards of a physical education teacher, man or woman, are of unusual importance. Of course, every teacher in the school is expected to exemplify the best in character and personal integrity. But there are circumstances in the physical education and athletic setting which give a little added emphasis to this necessity. In the first place, the physical education teacher is, like the band conductor and director of the glee club, more or less on public display part of the time.

Parents and the general public are likely to know him and be observant of his behaviour and conduct not only while he is on duty but in private circumstances as well. Surely, the coach attains something of the status of a public figure. What he does, opinions, he expresses, things he says, even the clothes he wear are noticed, and frequently imitated. There has always been a certain amount of hero worship associated with leadership in split, and both the man and woman physical education teacher may as well accept that as condition under which they work and turn it to the advantage of the students. Furthermore, the physical education teacher will meet a good many more people, perhaps, than will the silence teacher. The fans, the team followers, the personnel of press and radio, anxious parents, people from competing schools, representatives from professional sport, and in some instances gamblers and other curious characters who hang on to the fringe of the sport world will have to be dealt with. The teacher has to learn what can safely be said, how to say it and in general how to conduct himself in public life so that the students and the programme gain rather than lose from these contacts. There is still a third reason for the high premium on integrity in physical education. The budget for the programme is usually relatively high. Money is spent for equipment—

for hockey sticks and ear plugs, for helmets and hats. Moreover, money is charged for admission to games and festivals. The teacher has to learn early in life how to handle money, keep accounts, purchase equipment, and in general deal fairly and with scrupulous honesty in all such matters.

It is unfortunate when the physical education teachers gain the reputation of being somewhat exclusive and unwilling to work with others on the faculty. This exclusiveness seems to develop when the after-school activities keep the teachers away from faculty meetings or committee work, or when the rest of the faculty with muscular and not intellectual things. To avoid such a regard, physical education teachers' should attend faculty meetings as a matter of course, should be available for committee work, and should, in every way, represent the best in democratic participation and action within the school. Much of the criticism leveled at physical education, including athletics, comes from persons who are either uninformed or jealous of the prominence of the programme. The presence of the teachers at meetings attended by other staff members gives a chance for discussion.

Teachers of physical education must constantly remember they are teachers first and physical education teachers second. That is to say, the welfare of the total programme must constantly come before the welfare of any one area. In relation to administrative officials, such as the principal, superintendent, and board members, one should make every effort to cultivate a friendly informality developed within the traditional table of organization. The principal is in charge of the total programme, the superintendent of the system. These two officials must carry the responsibility, and thus the physical education teacher must work closely with them and he mindful of their relationship. Problems of curriculum, administration, or public relations can well be taken to the principal for discussion, and no physical education teacher should at any time assume the prerogative of administrative decision or policy making unless such right has specifically been designated as his.

The physical education teacher, because of his extraordinarily close relationships with students, must exemplify all that is fine in personal leadership. The teacher and the administrator will be scrutinized carefully for their energy, purpose, and personal integrity. The professional personnel need to be aware of ethical values, ethical bases for conduct. The that end the American Association for Health, Physical Education and Recreation has suggested a code of ethics for teachers of physical education, some of the principles of which are reproduced here:

1. Inasmuch as teachers of physical education are members of the teaching profession, the American Association for Health, Physical Education, and Recreation endorses without reservation the Code of Ethics for Teachers, adopted by the National Education Association.
2. In a democratic society every child has a right to the time of the teacher, the use of the facilities, and a part in the planned activities. Physical education teachers should resist the temptation to devote an undue amount of time and attention to the activities of students of superior ability to the neglect of the less proficient.
3. The professional relations of a teacher with pupils require that all information of a personal nature shall be held strict confidence.
4. To promote effective teaching, the teacher of physical education should maintain relations with associates which are based on mutual integrity, understanding and respect.

5. The physical education teacher should cooperate fully and unselfishly in all school endeavors which are approximately within the sphere of education. He should be an integral part of the school faculty.
6. It is an obligation of the teacher of physical education to understand and make use of proper administrative channels in approaching the problems encountered in education and in schools.
7. Professional ethics imply that altruistic purpose outweighs personal gain. The teacher, therefore, should avoid using personal glory achieved through winning team for the purpose of self-promotion.
8. It is considered unethical to endorse physical education equipment, materials and other commercial products for personal gain or to support anything of a pseudo-educational nature. Nor should a teacher profit personally through the purchase of materials for physical education by the school.
9. It is duty of every teacher of physical education to become acquainted with and to participate in the affairs of the community, particularly those concerned with making the community a better place in which to life. The teacher should take an active interest in the work of the various child-and-youth-serving agencies, participating as a citizen, and as a leader of children, youth and adults.
10. Inasmuch as physical education will programme through strong local state and national organizations, the teacher of physical education is obligated to membership and active participation in the proceedings of professional associations, both in general reeducation and in the specialized field of physical education.

Co-educational Progammes

After the primary years, and some times even during them, it has been considered unwise, or impractical, or immoral for boys and girls to have their physical education together. This custom has continued for nearly two centuries and has resulted in considerable duplication of programmes, facilities, and staff. It has been assumed that the sexes were so strikingly different in their social, psychological, and psychological makeups that there had to be developed a boys 'physical education and a girls' physical education. It has further been assumed that only a woman could teach girls and a man would be suitable for boys. Thus physical education is characteristically administered as a dual programme.

Analysis of the social life of the community and of the organic and psychological nature of man does not warrant such a divergence. Boys and girls play together, dance together, swim together in out-of-school life. They are interested in each other more or less continuously from kindergarten up. There may be a slight recession of interest at the junior high school level because of the earlier maturity of girls, but in the main our society requires that boys and girls associate with each other. Hence, the question arises: Whether better can children be taught to understand one another than through the experiences in physical education? By learning together, playing together, laughing together, they can learn to understand and respect the strength and weakness of each other.

Community life expects the sexes to intermingle. Bisexual experience is the base of the American home. Physical education has a great opportunity to make a contribution to community life by developing programmes which are coeducational in part. There are, of course, essential differences between the sexes, no suggestion that programmes be identical would be tenable. There are not sufficient differences. however, to warrant the complete separation of the two programmes. They can and should meet on many places of common ground. Activities such as dance in all of its forms, tennis, swimming, boating, winter sports, badminton, skating, riding, camping, softball, and others are particularly suited to coeducational participation on the upper levels. Virtually all of the games and dances of low organization are useful for mixed groups on the lower age levels.

The application of principles of democratic administration to class organization in physical education has altered former practices materially. A whole new concept of what a physical education class is or can be has developed out of efforts to think through the relationships of the individual to the purpose of physical education. The result has been a steady trend away from the large groups participating in mass activities toward smaller classes where as much individual attention as possible may be given and each person is an actively participating member and not just a member on the floor or a body to be exercised. Fifty years ago classes of fifty or a hundred or even more were not uncommon. When exhibition time came in the spring, several such classes would be combined and five thousand youngsters would entertain the inactive and sedentary spectors with routine drills based upon the central European conception of physical training. The impact of the democratic notion upon any such mass exercise s was clear, immediate, and resounding. They have been virtually eliminated from American physical education. By and large, physical education has responded to the democratic plea to "know your students." They are thought of as individuals, dealt with as personalities, guided as distinct persons, each with his own set of values, ambitions, and ideals. Such a transformation, from an exercising process to a learning and developmental experience, has been significantly responsible for the meaning which is implied in physical education.

Public Participation

School and college sport programmes hold great fascination for a segment of the public which find in them pleasurable outlets and good entertainment. This interest engenders the so-called "pressures" under which some coaches work. The more intense the pressure, the more difficult it is to maintain one's stability and purpose. The temptations to side with vested interests, to play favourites, to grant special privilege, to resent criticism, to lose one's temper, are all very real. The integrity of anyone within physical education may be measured in relation to the way he handles difficult situations. There are some in the field who genuinely enjoy the prominence of their position. They react to it with great modesty, with humility and good sense. Others artificially create a reputation as a showman. They conduct themselves as prima donnas, expect fanfare and trumpets when they appear on the stress or in assembly, act the fool on the bench with their protests and grimaces, and generally manifest a pitifully moronic type of exhibitionism. A physical education teacher can analyze his own reactions in this regard and must early decide whether he wishes to be a professional workman in the field of human development or a vaudeville clown with no concern for human values beyond "the gate" and the score.

Physical education is a field which is dynamic, not static. It moves forward. New ideas are constantly coming to the front. Research is productive, Experimentation with different ideas, different organizational plans, different methods, new equipment, goes on constantly. Revelations about child development, about the role of creative activity, about the effect of play on mental health, and other elements are worth following. Ideas are exchanged at professional meetings.The literature of the field contains reports of recent advances in all aspects of the programme. Correlative areas such as the social sciences, anthropology, and physiology are constantly throwing light on problems associated with physical education. No student of physical education can afford, either morally or intellectually, to slacken his interest in the scholarly aspects of his field. He must keep up with the literature, attend meetings, and generally be alert and informed about his profession.

10

Guidelines for Effective Physical Education

Physical education curriculum needs to focus on basic skills by having students participate in many types of age appropriate activities. As their skills develop, students can begin to understand that correct practice will result in improved learning and development of competency. They can become involved in activities that will assist in their own learning and help them begin to appreciate individual differences in their peers.

It is important for planners and instructors to become aware of the total experience of a comprehensive system across age groups. A well-planned physical education programme takes account of the long-term goals. Teachers of primary students are aware, for example, that students are moving toward the ultimate goal of making independent choices about physical activity in their teenage years. In addition, the element of pleasure in physical activity and an emphasis on pleasurable play should be a continual focus of physical education.

Physical Education at Nursery Schools

Children at nursery schools are solo learners. They focus primarily on moving within space, including the general space around them and their own personal space. Nonlocomotor skills include how the body moves on its axis, and locomotor skills include moving in general space. Once the children are able to move effectively in their space, they focus on objects-for example, equipment, supplies, and materials. They also learn about and interpret their environment through play. They should move in a safe environment that helps them look forward to positive experiences in physical education.

At this stage children can be guided to move in their environment for the sheer enjoyment of exploring space and controlling their bodies. They learn basic movement skills, including creeping, crawling, walking, hopping, and galloping on the preferred foot, playing rhythmic games and song games, and participating in circle or partner walks and marches. Nonlocomotor movement experiences include balancing, bending and stretching, twisting and turning, beating and shaking, tensing and relaxing, pushing and pulling, rising and falling, and participating in rhythmic and play activities that require those movements.

Children in kindergarten also learn the concept of static stability by experiencing various balances that position the center of gravity over the base of support. They learn that the body is in a stable, balanced position when the center of gravity is directly over the base of support and that improvement occurs when a skill is practiced many times. Object manipulation includes opportunities to manipulate and play with a wide variety of objects: lightweight balls, soft objects, beanbags, ribbons, hoops, and such student-made objects as sock balls, for example. At this stage students also perform free exploratory movement to rhythmic or musical accompaniment that is prerecorded or provided by the teacher or other students. The kindergarten experience begins with the expansion of knowledge of the physical self through identification of body parts-both external and internal. The kindergarten child's energy level and readiness to move contribute to a willingness to participate in aerobic-type activities. Through these activities students discover that the heart beats faster and breathing accelerates as they move their bodies. Learning about the importance of nutrition can begin at this level with instruction on selecting nutritious snack foods.

As kindergartners use their bodies to perform varied movements, they develop their own body image. Because self-image can be enhanced through movement experiences in physical education, children at this stage need many opportunities to experience personal feelings of success and achievement through movement. Children in kindergarten tend to play alone in their own space. They are focused on themselves in the present. However, they also begin to recognise the concept of self and others; acknowledge that others may occupy their space; learn to move about in their space without interfering with others; and begin to learn to take turns and share in interaction with others. Children at this stage generally do not understand the purpose of rules but will follow rules delivered by adults. The student will be able to:

— Travel in different ways in a large group without bumping into others or falling.
— Balance while bending, twisting, or stretching.
— Strike a stationary ball with any part of the body.
— Identify various parts of the body and their location-for example, arms, legs, and hands.
— Recognise changes in heart rate.
— Follow adult-delivered rules.

Physical Education at First Standard

Students at this stage expand their movement skills to

include qualities of space and time by learning to move in different directions at varying speeds. They explore a variety of movements, such as high-low and fast-slow. They also learn to recognise the element of time in movement -for example, how long it takes to move from one place to another and how long it takes an object to travel from one place to another. Through movement experiences first graders develop an awareness of the concepts of space, time, and effort. These experiences should include many opportunities for children to feel the joy that results from having the ability and freedom to explore, discover, and express themselves through movement.

As they continue motor learning, first graders accept challenges to move through space with the added dimensions of time and effort, such as fast-slow and strong-weak. Direction in movement is introduced along with basic eye-hand and eye-foot manipulative skills. Locomotor activities include hopping on the nonpreferred foot; galloping on the nonpreferred foot; and marching, sliding, and performing other patterns according to specific rhythms. Nonlocomotor movements include symmetrical and asymmetrical balances, lifting and carrying, starting and stopping, swinging, swaying, curling, and stationary dodging.

Students make deliberate moves in specified directions. They learn the biomechanical principle of dynamic stability. That is, balance is inherent in all movement, and individuals can increase their static stability by widening their base of support and lowering their center of gravity. They also learn that movement begins when their center of gravity moves to the edge of their base of support, their center of gravity is raised, and their base of support is narrowed. For example, a student is running, comes to a stop to maintain balance, and resumes running.

Students begin to manipulate objects with purposeful movement and learn to roll, toss underhand, bounce with two hands, retrieve, stationary-kick, and strike with the hand various objects that are safe and non-threatening. Simple dances in columns and circles and basic partner dances are appropriate at this level.

Although the child's movement becomes more purposeful and performance more deliberate, the instructor should encourage interest in the performance of an activity rather than any particular level of achievement. Especially at the beginning of the year, the physical education programme should include familiar and enjoyable games and activities that allow for each child's full participation.

First graders learn about the body's need for oxygen and food as fuel to supply the body with energy. They also learn about the role of the circulatory system in moving oxygenated blood to the muscles. They reflect on how their bodies feel as they experiment with different types of movement-for example, differing periods of time and types of space. The relationship of nutrition and exercise to physical strength and energy should be introduced at this level.

Children at this stage begin to form a personal body image through comparison with others. They learn that the body undergoes marked changes in height and weight and that those changes influence the movement and coordination of body parts.

First graders participate in parallel play with other students and tend to be more involved in individual activities than in interaction with others. They continue to learn in groups but participate as individuals. Multicultural experiences should be interwoven as appropriate-beginning in grade one and continuing through each level. The student will be able to:

— Travel and change direction quickly in response to a signal.
— Travel in relationship to objects: over, under, behind, and through.
— Place the body and limbs in different positions, demonstrating high, middle, and low levels.
— Toss and catch a ball alone or with a partner.
— Learn to use equipment safely and responsibly.
— Begin to recognise changes in his or her body, such as changes in height and weight.
— Develop responsibility for expected behaviours on the playground and in the classroom.

Physical Eduation at Second Standard

At this stage students explore movement patterns with a partner to define movement in relation to another person, shape, or group. They learn by continuing to experience a variety of modalities, including kinesthetic learning. Since the students are highly flexible in interacting with partners, activities should encourage changes of partners. In the application of rules, fairness at this stage is flexible, and children are likely to make up their own rules as they play together.

Total physical response-response with the entire body-occurs in motor movement as the student learns to define movement in relation to another person, shape, group, or group shape. Locomotor patterns include leaping and skipping, dancing with a partner, and dancing in a double circle. Nonlocomotor movements include dynamic balancing, dodging while moving, pantomiming, and mirror moving. To understand movement and apply laws of motion at higher grade levels, students learn to describe movement and differentiate among speed, velocity, and acceleration.

With partners second graders are able to compare various speeds and velocities. For example, students can talk about how fast they can run or walk and the difference between running and walking and other modes of locomotion.

Manipulative skills include catching a rolled ball; throwing and catching after one bounce; and kicking a stationary ball in a variety of ways. In addition to physical practice, students at this level should be encouraged to begin to use visualisation and mental practice to reinforce learning. The study of exercise physiology considers how the heart and lungs work as partners in cardiorespiratory health. In pairs students monitor the pulse at rest, during exercise, and after exercise. As they participate in movement that accelerates breathing and pulse rate, they learn the concept of the body's need for exercise to accelerate breathing and pulse rates on a regular basis. Nutrition, with a focus on foods healthy for the heart, is another factor in developing students' knowledge and skills related to cardiorespiratory health. Growth rates vary during this stage. As the children's awareness of others increases, they are able increasingly to see themselves in relation to others. They are also able to recognise and appreciate their own positive and negative feelings and those of others.

In grade two children learn more about relationships between themselves and others. They move from the sense of self in isolation and begin to embrace the concept of we and partners. This is also a time when children's growing awareness of others can help to promote knowledge of individual differences and different cultures. That can be the springboard, in turn, for encouraging children to accept and appreciate differences in others. The children are able to celebrate the successes of others and begin to recognise specific activities that contribute to feelings of joy and movement experiences that rely on cooperation. They consistently practice sharing and caring skills when playing with partners in movement activities and reinforce one another by giving and receiving encouragement. The student will be able to:

— Move backwards and change direction quickly and safely without falling.

— Jump and land, using a combination of one- and two-foot takeoffs and landings.

— Throw a ball hard, demonstrating an overhand technique, a side orientation, and opposition.

— Jump a self-turned rope repeatedly.

— Skip, hop, gallop, and slide.

Physical Education at Third Standard

Reacting and responding to others take precedence at this stage. By now students have a self-image strong enough to tolerate differences in how others react to them and are better able to make well-defined combinations of movements. Groups should never number more than five, the number that provides everyone with many turns and allows for natural leaders and followers to emerge. Students' motor ability increases as they gain greater control. They begin to develop a concept of the order of a sequence in movement and willingly experiment with and explore alternative movements. Third graders learn a variety of rhythmic patterns and gradeappropriate dances, using specific movement patterns, such as step-hop, step-swing, and two-step. Nonlocomotor skill development focuses on balance, including the use of apparatuses, inverted balances, balance on various body parts, and partner balances.

Students are able to describe muscular movement as the internal force that causes the body to change from a stationary to a moving object. They can also describe gravity, friction, and muscular movements as the external forces that cause the body to stop. They learn that specific types of movement provide benefits not only in developing skills but also in developing and maintaining health fitness. Striking skills, such as dribbling and volleying, continue to be refined. Students are also able to discriminate among cues, adjust to cues, and determine appropriate movements for specific situations. This stage foreshadows the marked physical changes that will take place in later childhood. The exercise physiology experience for grade three includes an emphasis on the importance of aerobic exercise for cardiorespiratory health, including the principles of warming up before exercising and cooling down afterward. In keeping with the grade-level emphasis on continuity and change, students participate in warm-up exercises to change the body to a readiness state for more vigorous exercise. In extended periods of aerobic activity, they also experience continuity of effort in cardiorespiratory conditioning. A third healthfitness component, flexibility, is emphasized during the warm-up and cooling-down phases.

Third graders begin to express themselves by creating new movement patterns involving time, space, and flow. They continue to celebrate successes and identify activities contributing to feelings of joy through active play.Students learn through play to handle individual responsibilities and resolve personal differences, becoming more capable of working together for a common goal as they grow in their ability to cooperate and take turns. The teacher should encourage the formation of groups of mixed gender during structured sessions because at this level boys and girls tend to separate for free play. During this stage students begin to gain respect for other classmates and for the property of others, understand different types of play, and assist each other by practising with a partner the rules of fair play. They learn to listen to each other and to react and respond appropriately. The student will be able to:

— Combine locomotor and nonlocomotor movements, such as combining various travel patterns in relation to music.
— Dribble a ball continuously, using the hands or feet to control it.
— Maintain flexibility by combining shapes, levels, and pathways into simple sequences.
— Recognize similar movement concepts in a variety of skills. For example, an underhand movement can be used in a variety of ways.
— Accept the feelings resulting from challenge, success, and failure in physical activity.
— Play and assist others in activities in groups of three to five.

Physical Education at Fourth Standard

Fourth graders are at a stage between childhood and youth during which they are growing in definite patterns. Eye-hand coordination is improved, and fine-motor activities are becoming more skillful. In addition, the greatest gain in strength begins at this stage. Students have mastered many locomotor and nonlocomotor skills and are able to manipulate objects in a variety of ways. They can create a game, for example, when they are given an object and encouraged to play. Physiologically, while they are standing, their center of gravity is still located in the midsection of the body, making balance and manipulation of objects a challenge. Fourth graders are likely to test rules during play and challenge how rules apply to them. Further, they tend to regard rules as rigid and prescriptive. When exceptions to the rules have to be made, the logic and rationale of the rules should be emphasized.

In motor development students at this level are able to focus on refining their skills in comparison with proficiency standards. They begin to use space and distance appropriately as they progress toward accuracy in throwing, catching, manipulating the body in space, and striking with body parts and objects-for example, volleying and dribbling a basketball with the hands and moving a soccer ball with the feet. They also learn about the concepts of projection-for example, applying greater force to an object to make it travel farther and knowing how to generate force by maintaining firm contact with the ground when the object is released.

Rhythmic activities include specific dances that may be related to the history-social science curriculum, such as dances appropriate to specific regions, ethnic groups, and cultures. Students also learn that there are many ways to learn and practice movement skills and that a practice session can be conducted in a variety of ways. Whole practice involves learning an entire sequence of movements that combine into a complex skill pattern; partial practice involves concentrating on one fundamental movement. Some skills may be introduced whole, learned in parts, and then practiced whole. Fitness-conditioning activities focus on various types of health-fitness exercises and many ways to combine those exercises into an exercise programme.

Another focus is on how physical exercise conditions the heart, lungs, and muscles. Students learn to differentiate between aerobic exercises that provide cardiorespiratory benefits and those that do not. They also learn about the importance of muscular endurance and strength as components of fitness. The role of nutrients in forming body composition and providing the energy needed to sustain physical movement should also be emphasized. At this level students are ready to cope with success and failure and are more perceptive and accepting of similarities and differences. This is also a time for developing, in the individual and in the group, wholesome attitudes toward victory and defeat. Appreciation of different styles of movement and the uniqueness of movement in various cultures begins to occur. Thus, fourth graders appreciate a sense of personal uniqueness in movement and become aware of the similarities and differences between themselves and others.

Fourth graders are ready to take the initiative within the group and demonstrate leadership as well as learn to be a good follower. This level is appropriate for the introduction of more complex games that challenge and increase performance abilities and enhance social skills. Fourth graders are able to cooperate with a partner in using equipment and helping one another improve object manipulation skills. Working together as part of large groups, they begin to appreciate personal differences and value the rights of others. They want to follow rules; thus, they need to learn to cope with conflicts and disputes by practicing conflict-resolution skills. The student will be able to:

— Leap, leading with either foot.

— Hand-dribble and foot-dribble a ball while moving within a group.

— Jump and land for height and distance.

— Maintain continuous aerobic activity for a specified time.

— Describe healthful benefits that result from regular participation in physical activity.

— Recognise the fundamental strategies in simple games.

Physical Education at Fifth Standard

At this level students continue to manipulate a variety of objects according to more specific goals. Now accuracy and speed, with a focus on targets, become important. Eye-hand, eye-foot, and other forms of coordination begin to come together. Fifth graders try continually to improve their motor skills, celebrate their successes and achievements, and take pride in individual excellence. Groups are expanded to include more than five students, and cooperative learning parallels that of other academic subjects. At this level the concept of fairness is emphasized. Students may be willing to change rules in order to achieve fairness for all.

At this stage specific body types are more efficient in certain movements, skills, and activities as body size and strength increase steadily. As students continue to improve in motor performance, they become more proficient in basic skills, such as running, jumping, and throwing. The ten-year-old begins to concentrate on the development of selective motor skills. Fifth-grade students manipulate objects through space with accuracy and with the added element of speed. As they practice for skill and accuracy, students learn that the desired expectation determines the type of practice needed to achieve that goal. One type of practice may be to concentrate on improving speed, another on improving accuracy, and still another on improving both.

In the application of Newton's second law, students experiment in throwing different sizes of balls, discovering that smaller objects will travel farther than heavier objects when the same amount of force is used. When speed is the objective, they learn to use a flat trajectory. They learn that to catch an object, they must increase

— the distance through which the object moves after contact; or

— the size of the area that absorbs the force of the object.

In grade five students examine the role of the circulatory system and its relationship to overall health. They are taught to develop strength and flexibility, including the interaction of strength and flexibility with the ability to perform forceful movements or manipulate objects with force. Further, they are taught how to maintain a healthy body by balancing food intake with physical activity and regulating the ratio of lean to fat body tissue.

Students at this stage learn to establish goals and select the practice techniques appropriate to the most immediate goals. They play gamelike activities in which the use of more than two skills to achieve objectives in the game is emphasized. Experiencing individual satisfaction increases at this stage as a motivational factor for future participation in a variety of activities. Increasingly, fifth-graders are able to use the body in movement to communicate feelings and to appreciate the aesthetic aspects of physical performance and the pleasure of achieving goals they have set for themselves.

Fifth graders thrive in small-group activity in which three to five students interact in cooperative play. They assume increasingly complex roles in cooperative activities; begin to develop an awareness of individual differences related to gender, cultural heritage, ethnicity, and physical ability; and appreciate the positive aspects of diversity. Social and game patterns include one against two, two against three, and two against two in activities such as goaltending. Students are beginning to recognise offensive and defensive play and understand that strategy is a skill to be developed within the context of play and games. Fifth graders know how to apply rules and demonstrate a sense of fairness in games and activities. Contemporary music and dance are popular.

PHYSICAL EDUCATION AT SIXTH STANDARD

Students at this stage are able to combine various skills in cooperative activities and give appropriate feedback to others. More independent in thought and action than younger students, they are also more likely to seek out new challenges in individual and group activities. Despite their desire for independence, however, sixth graders are likely to be genuinely interested in helping others. Because their interest in team play and organised games is strong, learning experiences can focus on developing the skills required for cooperative effort toward a common goal.

Students at this level are ready to combine skills for practice in lead-up games. These activities facilitate the learning of physical skills while allowing for cooperative effort. A unit should be included in sixth grade on cooperative games that can be used as lead-up games for more traditional sports. Juggling, unicycling, pogo-stick activities, bowling, foot-bag skill games, and throwing activities add variety and challenge as students improve their eye-hand and eye-foot coordination. This is also an appropriate time to add tumbling to previously learned stunts. Students learn concepts related to Newton's third law. That is, when struck, an object will rebound in the opposite direction with the same amount of force with which it is hit. The harder an object is hit, the greater will be the force that causes the object to rebound in the opposite direction.

A child's development, which is influenced by heredity, hormones, nutrition, and exercise, is also influenced by cultural expectations and gender differences. Students should understand that the achievement of certain levels of physical skill is dependent on all of these factors and that they should accept individual differences. Sixth graders are beginning to understand the purpose of each health-fitness component and the interrelatedness of all the fitness components in the development and maintenance of optimum health. Special emphasis should be given to the interaction of the circulatory and respiratory systems in conditioning for health fitness.

Students at this stage are able to recognise stylistic differences in performance, develop a more realistic self-image, and form collective attitudes as members of a group. They also begin to value looking good more than ever before as they become more aware of the varying levels of physical development within their peer group. Despite the physiological differences that occur at this age, students are generally willing to work cooperatively toward a common goal because desire for recognition within the group is strong. The physical education experience should foster in each student a sense of acceptance and belonging and of being valued within the group or on a team.

During lead-up games students at this level begin to recognise the validity of rule application and to accept that fairness applies to all. The grouping patterns for games can increase in size to six players. In keeping with the grade six history- social science focus on ancient civilisations, it is appropriate to introduce students to tribal dances and ethnic dances of contemporary or ancient cultures. Examples include the Pata Pata from South Africa, the Hora from Israel, and the High Life from Ghana.As students work in cooperative groups, they learn to provide one another with feedback and support in skill execution. They learn through experimentation that specific, positive, corrective feedback improves skill development more rapidly than general, negative, or neutral feedback and that the more promptly feedback is given after performance, the more meaningful the feedback is. Cooperation includes interacting with opponents in competitive activities to facilitate mutual development of skills. Sixth graders can accept and respect the performance of others, regardless of ability level, and are able to interact positively with others to develop friendships and participate in peer coaching activities with a partner.

PHYSICAL EDUCATION AT SEVENTH STANDARD

A well-planned physical education programme takes into account the importance of the transition from sixth to eighth grade and the rapid physical, social, and emotional changes occurring at this level. Students are beginning to look for a sense of belonging, community, peer group, and team even as they are gaining more confidence in individual activities. They have an eagerness to test themselves, both individually and in groups. This is an appropriate time to introduce individual risk taking and individual sports rather than focus exclusively on team sports.

Students at this stage tend to enjoy risk-related activities. Unless the school curriculum provides such activities in a safe environment, the students are likely to pursue the activities on their own without supervision. Appropriate activities include aquatics; combatives; tumbling; gymnastics; individual and dual sports; and outdoor education, such as adventure-based activities and orienteering. Specific adventure-based activities might include problemsolving exercises in which students work in small groups to solve physical challenges; trust falls; low-rope activities, such as balancing on a log suspended above the ground; high-rope activities in which students are involved in repelling or rock climbing; and rollerskating, skateboarding, and cycling. The tumbling unit introduced in grade six can be extended at this level to include apparatus for gymnastics and rhythmic gymnastics.

Seventh graders should learn more about the principles of spin and rebound. Spin results when force is applied off the center of an object. Students should become familiar with and begin to experiment with spins of various types: counterclockwise, clockwise, backspin, and topspin. They should learn how spin can be used to gain strategic advantage by players who understand how to apply it. Dance should include folk dances and other dances from cultures around the world to help students develop greater understanding and acceptance of their own heritage and that of others. As for motor learning, students at this level should understand that performance is measurable in terms of technique, accuracy, distance, and speed. They should be able to chart their own motor skill development in specific activities and events.

Seventh graders are also able to understand the interrelationship of the health-fitness components in the development of optimum health and thus to select specific exercises for each component. This is an appropriate time to introduce the FIT guidelines for physical exercise, which are the appropriate frequency, intensity, and time required for benefits to be accrued in each health-fitness component. Students should learn the principles of overload, progression, and specificity in physical conditioning.

Students' growth rates vary considerably during this period of development. Many experience their most rapid growth, and an increasing number show signs of puberty. All need to be aware that they must continue strenuous activity to maintain strength, speed, and endurance as their bodies change. They should study the impact of such factors as exercise, relaxation, nutrition, stress, and substance abuse on the body's ability to participate in physical exercise and on general well-being. Screening for posture deviation is required of all seventh graders, and parents must be notified when further examination is recommended.

The seventh grader is entering a time when he or she is more likely than ever before to take on new challenges, solve new problems, and be willing to take new risks. Risk taking involves new challenges and learning opportunities-trying out new equipment and new ways to use old equipment. Risk taking is attractive to students both alone and with others. They should be given a variety of opportunities to experience controlled risks through such activities as planned outdoor adventure activities and ropes courses. Students are also more likely to accept the challenge of setting personal goals for improvement related to health fitness and performance skills.

Seventh graders are increasingly able to meet challenges, solve problems, and resolve conflicts within a group. They are more likely to express an appreciation for cooperation and fair play as they adhere to group rules. This is also a time when students develop confidence to overcome anxieties associated with attempting something new, making new friends, and beginning to accept their own limitations.

The student will be able to:

— Leap, roll, balance, transfer weight, bat, volley, hand- and foot-dribble, and strike a ball with a paddle, using mature motor patterns.

— Participate in vigorous activity for a sustained period of time while maintaining a target heart rate.

— Identify proper warm-up, conditioning, and cooling-down techniques and the reasons for using them.

— Describe ways to use the body and movement activities to communicate ideas and feelings.

— Accept and respect the decisions made by game officials-whether they are students, teachers, or officials outside of school.

— Become engaged in activities that provide for challenge, problem solving, decision making, and risk taking.

Physical Education at Eighth Standard

At this stage students are able to focus on a common group or team goal over the long term, working together to solve problems during group activities. The emphasis in physical education moves toward team sports, including defensive and offensive strategies. Students should be encouraged to continue participation in group activities because all aspects of the personal development of eighth graders, both physical and mental, are still evolving. By the end of the eighth grade, students should have experienced a wide variety of activities. Now they can begin to see relationships among sports skills. For example, they may learn the underhand pitch for softball in one unit and transfer that skill to the underhand serve in volleyball and the serve in badminton. They should also be encouraged to understand that in certain situations transfer of learning can have a negative effect, such as learning the forehand drive in tennis and then applying it to the forehand drive in badminton.

A comparison of the offensive and defensive techniques used in team sports should be offered to help eighth graders learn the basic principles of strategy. In addition, students should have the opportunity to continue in a tumbling/gymnastics unit and a dance unit. Group dances, such as square, round, and contemporary line dances with directional changes requiring group cooperation, are appropriate. In eighth grade students learn the principles of rotation. That is, to rotate an object, one must apply torque. They also learn that the closer the mass is to the axis, the greater the rotary velocity will be. Eighth graders have many opportunities to experiment with these concepts, particularly during the gymnastics unit.

Students learn that growth in height and weight alters the mechanical nature of performance and that motor performance is related to all measures of maturity. Eighth graders are able to begin to design personal plans for a healthy life-style. The importance of appropriate intensity in exercising should be emphasized as students learn to calculate their individual target heart rate for exercise and to understand the importance of cardiorespiratory conditioning. They should also be able to distinguish the health-related fitness components of cardiorespiratory endurance, muscular strength and endurance, flexibility, and body composition.

By eighth grade students should have developed skills needed to reduce stress. Their higher level of motor achievement provides a basis for establishing new personal goals that they can realistically attain. Students are able to accept responsibility for their behaviour and resolve individual and group conflicts. They are mature enough to recognise the difference between ethical and unethical behaviour and appreciate the importance of fair play, cooperation, and competition in team games, activities, and sports. They are also capable of playing on teams, making decisions, and solving problems associated with physical activities. Team games and team sports are of great interest and value to eighth graders of both genders because they help satisfy the students' need to feel a sense of belonging to a group.

The team-sports units should include the history, rules, and strategy of each sport. By this time students should understand that the rules are fair to all participants and allow for safe participation. They should also begin to generalise and understand that infringements of the rules involving other people are fouls; that infringements involving space equipment, or time are violations; and that it is through the manipulation and understanding of the rules that strategies develop.

Group affiliation assumes added importance at this level, with emphasis being placed on team participation, roles of group members, group loyalty, and the identification of ethical and unethical behaviour in group activities. Students begin to think of themselves as members of a team and learn to cooperate rather than dominate other team members in team and dual sports. They learn to identify and apply specific criteria for successful team participation and to lead and follow by sharing leadership positions.

The student will be able to:

— Explore introductory outdoor skills.

— Perform a variety of simple folk, country, and creative dances.

— Practice appropriate ways of learning new skills or sports on his or her own.

— Improve and maintain appropriate body composition.

— Describe long-term physiological, psychological, and other benefits that may result from regular participation in physical activity.

— Recognise in playing team sports that rules are fair to all and allow for safe participation.

— Understand how growth in height and weight influences the mechanical nature of performance in physical activities.

Physical Education at Ninenth Standard

This is a stage at which students are able to synthesize much of what they have learned in the earlier grades, including knowledge of human growth, development, and physiology. Individuals are able to coalesce as a team and focus on the needs and contributions of other team members beyond themselves. Affiliation, a feeling of being connected and involved, is of primary importance to ninth graders. Students develop a willingness to acknowledge and respect stylistic differences in performance. The ninth-grade physical education programme should encourage students to gain an appreciation of others' achievements, no matter how large or small, and to expand their ability to adapt to the needs of the group and demonstrate fairness toward all.

The major emphases of study in the ninth grade are fitness, team sports, gymnastics, and aquatics. In learning about fitness, the students become familiar with new concepts related to the physiology of exercise; become knowledgeable consumers in relation to fitness; and experience a wide variety of exercises for flexibility, muscular strength and endurance, and cardiorespiratory endurance. In team sports ninth graders should be encouraged to select a sport in which to specialise; learn the history, rules, and strategies of the sport; and become proficient in the appropriate skills. The gymnastics unit should be an extension of the earlier tumbling and gymnastics classes. Here, too, students should be encouraged to select an event in which to specialise. For those students who already demonstrate proficiency in swimming, classes in water polo, skin diving, or advanced swimming can be offered. During an aquatics unit the students should learn the biomechanical principle of buoyancy. That is, to move efficiently through water, they must streamline their bodies to reduce the effect of drag. In addition, the swimmer's size, shape, surface, and speed of movement are factors affecting performance in swimming.

In grade nine the student is expected to develop an in-depth understanding of the components of total health fitness in a unit that emphasizes the physiological, psychological, and social benefits of a healthy, active lifestyle. Students should also begin to identify preferences for types of physical activity that can be pursued over the long term for fitness and recreation, including individual, dual, or team sports. Ninth graders should be able to explain the social, personal, and health benefits of developing skills in sports, games, and dance. They should be able to describe the aesthetic qualities of movement; feel good as they move efficiently and effectively; and develop the ability to evaluate personal needs, interests, and capacities that contribute to their movement choices.

In physical education experiences the ninth grader should demonstrate patterns of behaviour that reflect sound mental and emotional health, positive self-image, and acceptance of the total self. To help students achieve self-realisation through physical activity, the physical education instructor should guide the student's choice of fitness programs and activities to ensure a healthy lifestyle throughout life. Each student should set personal goals for health and fitness, including goals for improving health through physical exercise.

Ninth graders have the capacity to demonstrate mature teamwork by successfully resolving conflicts within the group. They should learn to cooperate in teamwork and in competition, analyse situations, find solutions to problems, obey rules, work for delayed rewards, and persevere toward a goal. The ninth grader is becoming increasingly more interested in sports as both participant and spectator. This increased interest is associated with several factors in addition to physical conditioning. For example, students have more choices in transportation and consumer spending. And they are bombarded with advertisements for all types of participant and spectator sports.The student will be able to:

— Analyse offensive and defensive strategies in games and sports.

— Participate in an individualised fitness programme.
— Identify and follow rules while playing sports and games.
— Identify ways in which rules are more alike than different and describe the difference between violations and fouls.

Physical Education at Tenth Standard

Students at this stage are capable of choosing the physical activities they want to pursue. They are more able to generalise from previous experiences and to apply biomechanical principles to the analysis of a variety of movement skills. A well-planned physical education programme will offer students a wide variety of opportunities. It will focus on individual or team sports of choice, dance, and personal defense, among other activities.

The five emphases of study for the tenth grade are individual and dual sports, outdoor education, combatives, dance, and analysis of movement. The individual or dual sport may be of the student's own choosing and may include such outdoor activities as orienteering, rock climbing, backpacking, and skiing. A personal defense class meets the combatives requirement and teaches students to avoid dangerous situations while preparing to defend themselves. The dance unit can be an extension of units taught at earlier grade levels. It can also be an elective that allows students to specialise in a specific type of dance at an intermediate or advanced level.

The analysis-of-movement class should conclude grade ten whenever possible. Reviewing what they have learned throughout the kindergarten through grade ten physical education curriculum, students should explore the reasons for physical education being taught in school, including the relationship between physical education and personal and social development. This class should also prepare students to be informed consumers in physical and recreational activities they plan to pursue outside of school. By the end of this unit, students should have developed a lifetime plan for physical fitness and activity. At this grade level students demonstrate improved performance, in part because their perceptual feedback has improved. They have acquired skills that are basic to efficient movement. In addition, they should have acquired a high level of physical fitness. They should be able to analyse the physiological and mechanical principles involved in human movement and make adjustments in physical exercise to achieve personal goals for fitness or motor performance or both.

The application of the principles of levers to movement should be introduced in tenth grade. The human skeletal system is made up primarily of third-class levers. Because the force arm (muscle) for human beings cannot be lengthened, the students should learn that in order to increase the force at impact with an object, they must strengthen the muscle or lengthen the striking element to increase the force. Students can apply these concepts in activities such as golf and tennis.

The awareness tenth graders have of the importance of commitment and dedication in physical education contributes to their desire to pursue excellence in a variety of ways-socially, emotionally, and intellectually. The tenth-grade physical education curriculum should emphasise that while learning any new skill, individuals go through three stages of learning:

(1) the cognitive phase;

(2) the practice phase; and

(3) the automatic phase, in which skills can be performed without concentrated attention.

Although moving through this cycle takes time, students at the high school level are mature enough to reach the automatic phase in selected skills. Tenth-grade students should be encouraged to evaluate the potential benefits and risks of available exercise programmes in the school and the community and the cost-effectiveness of exercise programmes offered to students as consumers. Each student should plan a personal exercise programme that is physiologically sound and appropriate to his or her needs, interests, level of ability, and goals for health fitness.

Tenth graders are often ready to assume leadership roles. By serving as peer coaches, they can take the initiative to assist other students by analysing their application of the principles of biomechanics and by providing feedback and suggestions for improvement. As they become more concerned with social etiquette, they can study the ways in which society's rules are expressed through games and sports. In addition, they can develop an awareness of the ways in which society influences their choice of lifestyle as to types of physical activity and the degree of their participation in physical activity in and out of school. Students at this level also develop an appreciation of movement as an art form that reflects cultural values. The student will be able to:

- Demonstrate basic competence in physical activities selected from each of the following categories: aquatics; self-defense; dance; individual, dual, and team activities and sports; and outdoor pursuits.
- Perform a variety of dances with fluency and in time to accompaniment.
- Use biomechanical concepts and principles to analyse and improve performance of self and others.
- Discuss the importance of balanced nutrition for a maintaining a healthy lifestyle.

— Design and implement a personal fitness programme that relates to total wellness.

— Participate in a variety of game, sport, and dance activities representing different cultural backgrounds.

— Discuss the historical roles of games, sports, and dance in the cultural life of a population.

— Acknowledge and respect stylistic differences in performance.

Physical Education at Plus Two Level

Students at this level continue to specialise in activities of their own choosing. In addition, they can pursue excellence in the activities they choose, following a specific regimen and honing specific skills. They are able to develop a personalised plan for lifetime fitness by assessing personal needs, interests, abilities, and opportunities in the area of fitness and by selecting activities that contribute to the achievement of personal fitness goals. They can also focus on combatives; outdoor education; aquatics; team sports and individual and dual sports of choice; tumbling; gymnastics; and dance. They can apply knowledge, skills, and attitudes acquired in physical education experiences from kindergarten through grade twelve to become proficient in one or more activities that lead to achieving personal goals for lifetime fitness. Schools should be encouraged to be creative in developing their physical education electives for these grade levels.

By the eleventh and twelfth grades, students are prepared to focus on the activities they plan to pursue after graduation from high school. They are able to explain why an individual's pursuit of excellence in any arena is an evolving process requiring commitment, courage, confidence, initiative, and perseverance. They have learned that self-expression through physical activity is of great value in developing and maintaining the healthy mind and body needed to excel in life. Students should be encouraged to select a variety of activities that correspond to their personal needs, interests, and capacities. They should also be encouraged to reassess their changing needs and interests continually as they grow and mature. Students should be encouraged to select activities in which they will continue to specialise. Therefore, the biomechanical principles they study should be directly related to the activities they select. The students should also be encouraged to apply their knowledge of exercise physiology in planning and pursuing lifestyles conducive to maintaining optimum health.

The senior high school student is at a stage where he or she can develop an increased interest in selecting activities in accordance with personal body type and capacities. By the eleventh grade students should have learned to evaluate personal performance in a variety of activities. They should be given the opportunity for self-direction in the selection of activities that can be enjoyed for health and fitness throughout life. Having selected activities for specialisation, the student should have the motivation to learn. Students should be aware that the learning process takes them through three stages of learning and should understand that they must repeat and practice skills in a variety of ways in order to achieve excellence. They should also know how to measure their performance at different stages to maintain their motivation and adjust their goals for future training.

By the eleventh and twelfth grades, students are prepared to focus on the activities they plan to pursue for recreation or a career after graduation from high school. Elective units in a wide range of activities should last for a sufficient period of time. Students who complete these classes should be well prepared to continue the activity on their own.

Students should be encouraged to work in small groups to provide one another with specific positive/corrective feedback so that individual excellence can be achieved. They should apply social skills acquired in physical education activities in preschool through grade twelve to enhance their own experience and the experience of others with whom they are involved in physical and social activities. They should also be encouraged to support and participate in community organisations that promote health and fitness by providing lifelong recreational opportunities for people of all ages.

The student will be able to:

Grade eleven:

— Use the principles of movement to accomplish a task with the least effort.

— Demonstrate some mastery of skills in games, sports, and dances and participate in intramural programmes.

— Comprehend the correct elements of various movements, strategies, safety procedures, and basic rules.

— Show evidence of developing and maintaining physical fitness to achieve the goal of a healthy lifestyle.

— Show evidence of a positive self-image.

— Share in the responsibility of group action and problem solving as a member of a group or team.

Grade twelve:

— Excel and continue in an activity of choice, such as a sport, dance, gymnastics, or aquatics.

— Demonstrate advanced competence in at least one activity from the curriculum.

— Be able to design and execute a physical fitness programme, recognising that changes in lifestyle may progress over time from vigorous activities to mild exercise, including walking.

— Accept the ways in which personal characteristics, performance styles, and activity preferences will change over the life cycle.

— Know about career opportunities in physical education and related fields.

— Evaluate critically the claims made in advertisements about commercial products and programmes.

Bibliography

Cureton, T.K., "The Physiological Effects of Exercise Programs Upon Adults, Springfield, IL: Thomas, 1969.

DeLorme, T., & Watkins, A., "Progressive Resistance Exercise", New York: Appleton-Century Crofts, 1951

Gordon, E.E., "Anatomical And Biomechanical Adaptations of Muscle to Different Exercises", *Journal of the American Medical Association*, 1967.

Grana, W. J. Lombardo, B. Sharkey, & J. Stone (Eds.) *Advances in Sports Medicine and Fitness* 45-59 Chicago: Year Book Medical, 1988.

Henry, F.M., "The academic discipline of physical education." Quest, 1978.

Hodge S.R., Davis R., Woodard R., Sherill C., "Comparison of Practicum Types in Changing Preservice Teachers' Attitudes and Perceived Competence." *Adapted Physical Activity Quarterly*, 2002.

Hogan, P.I., "Problem based learning and personnel preparation in adapted physical education", *Adapted Physical Activity Quarterly*, 1990.

Ikai, M., "Training of Muscle Strength And Power in Athletes", *Paper presented at F.I.M.S,* Congress, Oxford, England, 1970.

Jackson, J., Sharkey, B.J., & Johnston, L.P., "Cardiorespiratory Adaptations to Training at Specified Frequencies", *Research Quarterly*, 1968.

Kanehisa, H., & Miyashita, M., "Specificity ofVelocity in Strength Training. European Journal of Applied Physiology", 1983.

Lieberman, L.J., Houston-Wilson, C., "Strategies for inclusion: A handbook for physical educators", Champaign, IL: Human Kinetics, 2002.

Lienert, C., Sherrill, C., Myers, B., " 'Physical educators' concerns about integrating children with disabilities: A cross-cultural comparison", *Adapted Physical Activity Quarterly*, 2001.

Lohman, T.G., Roche, A.F., Martorell, R. (Eds.) "Anthropometric Standardization Reference Manual", Champaign, IL: Human Kenetics, 1991.

Lytle R.K., Collier D., "The consultation process: adapted physical education specialists' perception." *Adapted Physical Activity Quarterly*, 2002.

Massey, B.H., Nelson, R.C., Sharkey, B.J., & Comden, T., "Effects Of High Frequency Electrical Stimulation On The Size And Strength Of Skeletal Muscle", *Journal of Sports Medicine*, 1965.

Newell, K. M., "Physical activity, knowledge types, and degree programs", *Quest*, 1990.

Parffenbarger, R.S., "Physical Activity as an Index of Heart Disease in College Alumni", *American Journal of Epidermiology*, 1978.

Pollack, M.L., "The Quantification of Endurance Training Programs, In J.H. Wilmore (Ed.) *Exercise and Sports Science Reviews* (vol.1) New York: Acadmic Press, 1973.

Reid, G., Stanish, H. "Professional and disciplinary status of adapted physical activity". *Adapted Physical Activity Quarterly*, 2003.

Rink, J. E., "Teaching physical education for learning", St. Louis: Mosby, 1993.

Stanton, K., Colvin, A., "The physical educator's role in inclusion". 1996.

Sharkey, B.J., *Physiology of Fitness*, Campaign, IL, Human Kenetics, 1990.

Tesch, P., Thoresson, A.,& Kaiser, P., "Muscle Capillary Supply and Fiber Type Characteristics in Weight and Powerlifters", *Journal of Applied Physiology*, 1984.

Vorobyev, A.S., Prilepin, M.S., "Comparative Effectiveness of The Different Types of Loadings, Applied In The Weightlifters Training", *Vol 1 International Weightlifting Journal*, Sofia, Bulgaria, 1979.

Wenger, H., & Bell, G., "The Interaction of Intensity, Duration, and Frequency of Exercise Training in Altering Cardiorespiratory Fitness", *Sports Medicine*, 1986.

Index